The Elvis]

Beyond the headlines and ~~~
to the heart of the superstar

1970-1977

By
Robert C. Cantwell

Elvis Aaron Presley January 8, 1935-August 16, 1977

"I would have been duty-bound if I had recognized Elvis' alleged drug abuse."
Robert C. Cantwell

Elvis, Jody and Bob Cantwell in Las Vegas

ISBN-10:1-939217-82-2ISBN-13:978-1-939217-82-0
The Elvis Presley I Knew-Color Version
Robert C. Cantwell
Copyright Robert C. Cantwell 2013
Published by 5 Prince Publishing

Photo Credit: Front Cover Robert C. Cantwell
Author Photo: Robert C. Cantwell

First Edition/First Printing October 2013 Printed U.S.A.

DEDICATION

To my devoted wife, Jody, of 51 years and still going, who pushed me when I would had rather be do anything else, but sitting at a computer writing this book.

To our children, Dawna (Brent), Rob (Barbara) and Ron (Clare) who were getting tired of me asking them to critique what I had written.

To my grandchildren, Jyl, Greg, Lynda, Robert, Ryan, Reid, Annalise, and Katherine who encouraged me to record my times with Elvis Presley.

To the Denver Police Department (DPD) that kept my childhood dream alive giving me the opportunity be a member of Denver's Finest; the Colorado Bureau of Investigation that exposed me to the quality of the Law Enforcement Agencies serving and protecting Colorado citizens; and the Colorado Department of Corrections that is often overlooked for the extremely tough tasks they have managing inmates; and to all who worked for me and with me.

To Ari Zavaras, former DPD Chief of Police, Manager of Safety, Executive Director Colorado Department of Public Safety and Colorado Department of Corrections, for believing in me and advancing my Law Enforcement Career.

SPECIAL RECOGNITION

This book could not have been possible without the shared memories from my friends and long-time colleagues, Jerry Kennedy and Ron Pietrafeso.

Elvis, Bob, Jerry and Ron

SPECIAL RECOGNITION

Elvis Presley who left me a lifetime of unforgettable memories. Although he has left he continues to be alive in my mind and heart.

Jerry Kennedy an icon within the Denver Police Department and remains well respected even after his retirement as a Division Chief in 1991. Jerry is known and recognized for all the drug and organized crime busts he made. His wisdom and leadership skills developed many officers to be Denver's finest.

Ron Pietrafeso was undoubtedly the best-dedicated narcotic detective I knew. I was honored to work with him and call him a friend. I spent more time with Ron than I did my own family. He loved what he did and had no promotional ambitions, just to be the best "narc." His work ethic was unsurpassed and the quality and quantity of cases his team of narcs closed positioned DPD on the map as the best drug agency in the state. For his distinguished service, DPD awarded him the Medal of Honor. Ron left the department after 16 years for a successful business career.

I have encouraged Jerry and Ron to write their own accounts. They were with Elvis more than I was.

Acknowledgements

Bernadette Marie Giambrocco-Soehner, a publisher of numerous books, who unknowing to her or me when my wife (Jody) gave her a ride in the 'Yellow Cadillac' Elvis gave me, that she would one day publish my book on the "The Elvis I knew."

Joe Esposito, who continues to keep Elvis alive in the hearts of millions, young and old, and remaining a friend,

Elvis Presley Enterprise for their authorization for me to use the pictures I took at Graceland.

Denver Police Department providing the authorization to have DPD laboratory capture pictures of Elvis in 1970, 1971 and 1976, for Jerry Kennedy, Ron Pietrafeso and me.

Ron Wentz, former Federal Narcotic Agent, for taking his own time in 1970 to take pictures of Elvis.

Cindy Brovsky, a published author, for editing my initial book drafts.

Melanie Kirkley who put her "scissors" down to review a draft of my book and provide critique.

The Denver Post

The Denver Rocky Mountain News

Denver Westword

Denver Public Library
Memphis Press-Scimitar

The Commercial Appeal

John Porter Director of Ecommerce Mountain Valley Spring
Water Company

Ann Dinkins Customer Service/Procurement, Villiger Kiel
Cigars North America

Vail, Colorado Visitor Center

CONTENTS

INTRODUCTION

I must have heard a little birdie telling me many years ago to save everything. Having the pack rat nature I do, has been very instrumental in helping me to recall the many celebrities I have met. I would be certain that the most questions would be when DPD Sergeant Don DeNovellis convinced me to assist him in providing security for Mother Teresa, when she came to Estes Park, Colorado. No, the one I get the most questions about is Elvis Presley.

Me and Mother Teresa

My wife, children and grandchildren encouraged me to write down the memories of my time with Elvis from 1970-1977 while I was serving in the Denver Police Department. My date books, notes, photographs, saved newspaper articles, and stories retold to me by my former colleagues and friends, support these memories.

Elvis had everything that any poor boy growing up could only dream of having: a glamorous life and money. My own deprived childhood gave me a better basis than most for understanding and forming a true friendship with Elvis.

Since his death in 1977, there have been many books, magazines and newspaper articles written about the Elvis I didn't know.

The Elvis I knew was more than the world's superstar; he was a true country gentleman. He cherished those that treated him as a normal person rather than a meal ticket. Some who called Elvis "friend," were only his pals when they were on the payroll. Elvis once told me, "If I was 'down and out' they would drop me in a minute. I know you guys would still be here." He was right.

Elvis' life and tragic ending has been extensively covered in all forms of media. I wanted to share my memories of the man few people had the good fortune to witness firsthand. He was more than an amazing singer and entertainer. He was a generous, caring man who craved true friendship and loyalty.

Elvis has "left the building," but he never has left me.

PROLOGUE

Elvis 1970 in Denver

Why did Elvis Presley die unexpectedly on August 16, 1977 at the age of 42? Was Elvis apprehensive about appearing in public as an aging overweight sex idol? Was it an eerie coincidence that paralleled Elvis' unconditional love for the most important woman in Elvis' life, his mother, Gladys, who died at the age 46, on August 14, 1958? Was it truly medical issues and Elvis' over indulgence of prescribed drugs? Was Elvis' death brought on by two of his bodyguards after being fired by Elvis and then publishing, "Elvis: What Happened," (Red West, Sonny West and Dave Hebler: as told to Steve Dunleavy Ballantine Books 1977) graphically describing Elvis' unpredictable behavior and drug abuse?

Was it the Colonel who thought more about money and dominating Elvis and discarding Elvis' health issues?

We will never know. If you knew the Elvis I did, you would surmise it was a combination of the above.

From the first time I met Elvis on November 17, 1970, when he performed a concert in Denver, we would have conversations about his mother and he told me Red and Sonny West were like his brothers, since his only sibling, Jesse Garon died at birth.

Throughout my time with Elvis, with a few exceptions, and noticeably not at Elvis' funeral, Red and Sonny were nearby Elvis. I actually liked them both. But while they spent much more time with Elvis than I did, I can dispute one story they recalled that actually involved me.

Their assertion that two undercover Denver narcotic agents learned Elvis had a prescription for a heavy painkiller and started watching Elvis during his visit to Vail, Colorado in January 1976 is flawed. They said that the two narcotic agents confronted Elvis, but not for the reason they write.

When we left Vail, Elvis said he wanted to talk with me on why he gave me a Cadillac and what he expected from me in return. No doubt Elvis was very upset and with no apologies from either of us, Elvis gathered his pilots and stormed out of the hotel back to Graceland.

When reports of Elvis' drug usage were front-page news alleging this was the cause of his death, questions besieged Jerry, Ron and I that we should have recognized Elvis' drug usage. No question we would have. Good police officers, especially narcs, always have a full understanding and awareness of their surroundings, on or off duty. My wife calls me overly paranoid because I am suspicious of everyone including family members. Once I arrested my brother-in-law (now former) for drugs. My dad was committed twice to the VA hospital; once in Big Springs, Texas and once in Denver to withdraw from his addiction to drugs; that didn't work for my dad.

The only recollection where Elvis even remotely mentioned using any type of drug was when he said that he often would need to use "sleeping aids" to finally get to sleep. During the many conversations Elvis and I had he would tell me how he was totally against drug dealers and that the users were victims of these predators.

Any thoughts that I would look the other way because Elvis was a celebrity had no truth. I had arrested other entertainers for drug possession while working off-duty events in Denver. One was performing on stage when I saw him taking a white substance, what appeared to be cocaine, from a small vial and stuffing some up his nose. My partner, Ron Pietrafeso, and I snatched him off of the stage. The white powder tested positive for cocaine. The fans became unruly and it was not a very popular arrest with the promoter, who demanded I be fired.

Jerry supported me and told the promoter that Ron and I would work the outer perimeter at concerts. This was fine with me because I didn't like the loud music. Besides, we made more arrests outside before, during and after concerts.

I can honestly and unequivocally state that I never saw Elvis use or appear under the influence of drugs, nor hear anyone talk or express concerns that Elvis was using drugs. Because I was a cop maybe they were all extra cautious around me.

What happened at Graceland in 1977 was a great loss of a powerful entertainer. If I had any inkling of Elvis' drugs indulgence, I would not have looked the other way. He was definitely a transformed person when others were around him; acting out the persona that he felt was expected of him.

When I was asked to work off-duty for the Elvis concert, in Denver, November 1970, it initially was to be another paycheck to help supplement my income to support my family. Never would I have guessed that this one night of work would lead to seven years of lasting memories of the of "The Elvis I Knew."

Chapter 1
FIRST MEETING ELVIS
Tuesday, November 17, 1970

Elvis 1970 in Denver

I was thirteen and living a pretty rough childhood in the West Texas oil boomtown of Snyder when Elvis performed his first concert at the Denver Coliseum on Sunday, April 8, 1956.

Denver Coliseum then and now (Denver Public Library)

When Elvis returned to Denver fourteen years later on Tuesday, November 17, 1970, to perform for a sold-out concert at the same coliseum, I was now a six-year veteran and a proud member of the Denver Police Department (DPD), and a detective assigned to the Specialized Narcotics Unit (SNU), a statewide drug enforcement unit.

Elvis' popularity had spanned more than two decades. I listened mostly to his gospel music. I believe what set Elvis apart from other singers were the backup groups that complimented the quality of his music. Before I go any further, those who know me are aware my music tastes favors Gospel and country singers Ernest Tubb, Hank Williams, Patsy Cline and a few others, singing those tear jerking songs.

As I was preparing to work the Elvis concert as an off-duty officer, I wondered if the event was going to be like the numerous other rock concerts I had worked. I really didn't care for most, if not all, of the "rock concerts." The music was so loud and I couldn't understand a word they were singing, and I thought their attire was weird. The crowds they attracted were also questionable and often out of control. I made many arrests for drugs, not to mention the number of concertgoers who overdosed and had to be carried off.

Elvis was known for being "The King of Rock 'n' Roll" and I wondered whether this concert would just be more of the same.

Elvis' road manager was Joe Esposito. Elvis had met Joe in the Army when they were both stationed in Germany. Joe sought out the best hotel near the venue to accommodate Elvis and his entourage. They ended up at the Radisson Hotel, 1776 Grant St., which had the Playboy Club on the top floor.

Radisson Hotel (now the Warwick)

It was imperative and non-negotiable that Elvis and his entourage would occupy two entire floors and the rooms must be several floors above the hotel's main entrance for security purposes. Only Elvis and the very close-knit members traveling with him would occupy the 10th floor, along with the DPD Officers providing security. The band members would room on the 9th floor.

Jerry Kennedy was secondary work coordinator for DPD off-duty officers moonlighting. He scheduled off-duty officers for Elvis' security at the hotel and at the coliseum. It wasn't hard for Jerry to find off-duty officers to work the concert because they all wanted to see and hear Elvis, including me. But when Jerry had a harder time finding hotel security, Ron and I got the assignment, despite our protests of missing the concert we were assigned the security detail on the 10th floor, while a couple of other DPD officers were assigned the 9th floor. "The hotel position will be better anyway, and for once we will go home with clean uniforms on," I told Ron.

Frequently after working a concert we were dirty and smelly from making arrests and from the 'pot' cloud that hung over the inside of arenas. I thought this assignment would be relaxing since everyone would be at the concert and Ron and I could actually get some work done studying the mug shots we always carried of Denver's drug traffickers and organized crime family members.

I couldn't have been more wrong; there was nothing easy about the night ahead of us, except we had the once in a lifetime opportunity to personally meet and greet "The King."

The hotel staff strategically placed a desk with two chairs on the 10th floor hall in front of the elevator leaving just enough walking room for someone getting off the elevator. Jerry told Ron and me that we were responsible to keep all unauthorized people off of the 10th floor and only the names on the list that Mr. Esposito provided us were permitted on the 10th floor.

The list included Elvis.

It was early evening and a few hours before the concert began when the elevator door opened. Ron and I immediately stood up behind the desk. It was Elvis dressed in his signature black cape. He approached Ron and me and greeted us, shaking our hands.

Even though we recognized Elvis from pictures, I asked if we could see his ID.

"We can only let people on this floor who are on this list," I told him, carrying out my security duties.

Elvis' bodyguard then jumped in saying, "You know this is Elvis."

I countered that there had been several Elvis impersonators around town and we had to be sure.

Elvis said, "You're right officer, good job."

Ron and I checked each of Elvis' bodyguards' IDs hanging around their necks and their IDs looked similar to the one Joe Esposito had on. They were still unimpressed and re-assured us that this really was Elvis.

"Hell, my partner and I have never seen or met Elvis in person," I told the group. "And this may not have been the best way to actually meet him, but this is our job. One time we didn't check a person that was on a list and we got our ass in a jam."

Elvis again agreed we were just doing our job but even that didn't change his bodyguard's distaste for us.

Instead of just heading for his room, Elvis asked us about our jobs and he was intrigued when we told him we were narcotic detectives but generally wore our uniforms when we worked off-duty events.

He wanted to hear more about our work as narcs. This was the first time a celebrity was interested in our job and we jumped at the opportunity to share our war stories. Most celebrities we worked with snubbed police officers and acted like we should feel privileged to be in their presence, if they found out we were narcs they avoided us like the plague.

While Elvis continued talking to us, one of his bodyguards moved behind me and gazed down over my shoulders. The majority of police officers I know, including me, always make sure in restaurants–and other public places sit so our backs are not facing a door. It comes with the job of being on-guard for anything. Not to long ago three DPD Detectives were eating in a restaurant in Southwest Denver when it was being robbed. A shootout ensued and the robbers were caught in the act of their crime.

I looked up at the bodyguard and asked, "Please don't stand behind me."

Elvis abruptly turned toward his bodyguards and told them to go find their rooms and get some rest. Elvis told me later his men were not used to this kind of tight security. He laughed when I suggested they looked at us like we were a threat to their jobs.

I would later learn the men were part of what was called the "Memphis Mafia." We talked for a few more minutes before Elvis told us he was going to his room to relax before his concert.

It wasn't long before the elevator opened again and some guys looking like "hippies from the sixties" started to get off. Ron and I looked at each other and I said, "RP (I would often address him by his initials as I would Jerry) we thought tonight was going to be quiet."

We stood up from the desk and Ron proceeded to question them and advised them they couldn't be on this floor. In unison the group politely said they were members of Elvis' band and displayed Elvis concert TCB credentials. We told them they belonged on the 9th floor and they backed up into the elevator and very respectfully said thanks.

"Stereotyping again RC?" Ron said. I replied, "Yes, I think we will be making some drug busts tonight… and I thought Elvis' concert would be different."

Unknowingly to us, Elvis was standing at the corner next to the hallway. As he approached us I looked at him with an expression of, "Oh-shit he heard me!"

He told us his band members didn't use drugs. But since I had a concern, he was going to order them to leave their rooms doors open and he wanted us to later check each of their rooms, including his. "If you see or smell anything illegal you can arrest them and I will also fire them," Elvis said, before walking away.

I knew Elvis was not happy with what I said about his band members and I apologized to Ron for likely getting him into another mess. We both were quite sure Elvis would tell Jerry about the exchange. He did and soon Jerry and Joe Esposito stepped out of the elevator.

I made sure that our boss knew it was me and not Ron who caused the problem and asked, "Am I fired?"

Surprisingly, Jerry told us, "No, Elvis was stunned and thought it was a good idea. No one thought to say anything about these guys before."

When it was time for Elvis to leave, dressed in a white cape and diamond-studded jumpsuit for his concert, he came over and stood by Ron and me. Then it became clear why Elvis was considered a sex symbol. He was tall, dark and handsome, with a low appealing tone when he spoke that even Elvis impersonators have a hard time imitating.

I was ready to settle in for the night when Elvis asked our boss if Ron and I were going to the concert. Jerry explained we needed to watch the 10th floor but Elvis suggested the officers on the 9th floor take over for us while we were gone. And, as easy as that, we were going to the concert.

While we waited for an officer from the 9th floor to arrive, Elvis asked me if there was a special song I wanted him to sing at the concert. I told him my wife and I liked his version of "How Great Thou Art," but that it may not be appropriate for a concert. Elvis just smiled.

Soon we were on our way to the coliseum in a limousine.

"No one is going to believe this…I don't. I must be dreaming," I told Ron.

During the concert Ron and I sat on the edge of the stage and Elvis looked toward me when he sang "How Great Thou Art." It was undoubtedly better than all the other concerts I had worked and I could understand every word of his songs, even the ones I didn't like.

The crowd of fans, mostly young and older women, lined the stage screaming. It became necessary for Elvis' bodyguards and officers to come forward to keep them from jumping on the stage and grabbing Elvis. He walked around the stage and would take a scarf from around his neck that had been handed to him by his lead guitarist, Charlie Hodge. Elvis would wipe sweat from his forehead and then place the scarf around one of the lucky girls swaying her hands into the air close to the stage. More women would get scarfs and walked away crying.

Unlike at other concerts, the screaming girls attending Elvis' concerts were dressed conservatively and very respectfully. There also was no evidence of drugs usage at this concert, a first in my experience.

After we returned from the show, we realized the word was out where Elvis was staying because there were screaming women of all ages in and around the hotel lobby. They didn't see Elvis because we had brought him through the backside underground parking door of the hotel. Elvis was being constrained by his bodyguards, and they took Elvis hastily to his room.

Ron and I returned to our elevator duty, with Jerry and Esposito reminding us not to let anyone off the elevator.

Elvis' bodyguards walked over and told us EP (the nick name they used for Elvis) was safely in his room and they would see us in the morning. A short time later Elvis walked over and being a Southern gentleman, shook our hands and told us "thanks for everything" then went back to his room. Ron and I looked at each other, in disbelief that he took the time to thank us.

It was after midnight and we were kept busy holding the women back who kept trying to get off the elevator. Elvis came back again just as the elevator opened and when the load of women saw him they went nuts. Elvis waved at them as he hurriedly walked backward toward the hallway and around the corner so he couldn't be seen. Meanwhile, it took everything Ron and I had to push the women back into the elevator.

Once the elevator closed and before the next rush, Elvis came back around the corner. He told us he was expecting a nurse and that it would be okay to let her off and bring her to his room. He then quickly retreated back to his room.

About an hour later Elvis came back and asked me about the nurse.

"Elvis, someone must have told them what floor you were on," I explained. "There has been one full elevator after another loaded with women screaming and wanting off. I haven't seen any nurse and I would have recognized her if she had nurses' clothing on or identified herself as a nurse."

This would be the first time I saw Elvis lose his cool when he sizzlingly explained that it was not the typical "nurse" that was arriving. He called Jerry as well, but I told him we were just following orders not to let anyone off the elevator.

Because we had no clue what this "nurse" looked like, Elvis had Esposito station a couple of his bodyguards at the elevator with us. It wasn't long before they let two good-looking well-dressed women on to the floor and escorted them to Elvis' room.

With that drama over, I decided to follow up on Elvis' request to check the rooms on the 9th and 10th floors where the doors were left open. I did a visual search of the rooms and didn't find or smell anything. Several of the rooms were empty and I was told some of the band members were at the Playboy Club into the early morning hours, but that was none of our concern. I told Ron that I was going to check Elvis' room because it was only fair. Ron said go ahead but he was staying by the elevator. When I checked Elvis' room, the two women from the elevator were with him joking and laughing. I waved and swiftly left.

Elvis was fine with this, but his band members were not happy.

It was early Wednesday morning, November 18, when Jerry relieved me to go home, get some rest and change out of my uniform before returning to the hotel. I carried a camera back with me. I thought, "What the heck, I'm going to ask Elvis if I can take some photos."

Off-duty DPD Police Security Radisson Hotel November 18, 1970
Sgt. Bill Sailors, Me, Ron,
Dick Grob (one of Elvis' body guards) and Jerry

I figured I may never have another opportunity and I had nothing to lose if Elvis said no, but I would be prepared if he said yes. Ron had left for home and returned with a change of clothes. Jerry took a nap in the room that Joe had reserved for DPD police.

Elvis had admired Jerry's DPD lieutenant badge when he first met Jerry and told Jerry he wanted one. While Elvis slept, arrangements were made with DPD Chief of Police George Seaton to obtain Elvis a DPD lieutenant badge. It was all set up for Elvis before he finally got up. We were on Elvis' time.

On the way to DPD Headquarters, with Elvis, Charlie Hodge and Sonny West, I asked Elvis if it would be okay if I took some pictures. Elvis didn't hesitate with his response, "Yes, I would like that."

A big smile came to my face.

As soon as we arrived at the police building, Jerry made preparations to have police lab technician, Bill Smith, available to take photos because he was not going to take a chance with my old camera. I was glad because Bill was an expert photographer, but I still snapped some.

When the word got out that Elvis was in the building, DPD staff lined up to meet him. I was impressed that Elvis took time to shake hands with everyone he encountered on the way to the Chief's Office, led by Jerry.

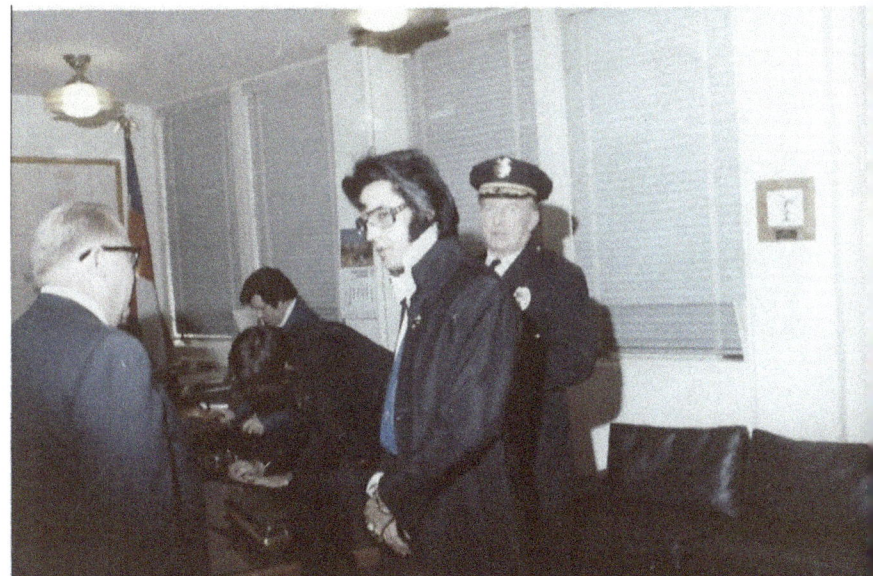

Chief Seaton, Elvis, Jerry, and Charlie Hodge
being fingerprinted at DPD 1970

Elvis was very excited when he heard he would go through the same process as any person who applied to the DPD. He would first be fingerprinted and then have his mug shot taken. While both of those were done for Elvis and his bodyguards without a hitch, Elvis was disappointed when the Chief presented him with an honorary lieutenant badge. Catching his error, the Chief exchanged the honorary badge for a real badge.

Elvis' face lit up like a kid when he saw the real badge and they shook hands while the cameras caught the historical moment.

Ron, Rusty Mitzner, Elvis, Jerry, and Chief Seaton 1970 at DPD

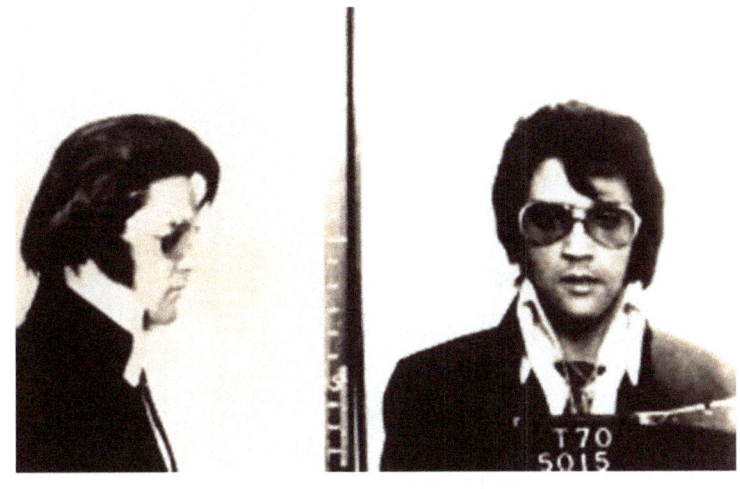

On the way back to the hotel, Ron asked Elvis if he could invite a few fellow narcs over for more photos. Elvis readily agreed because he wanted to show us his guns. Again, we wanted a good photographer, so Ron called BNDD (Bureau of Narcotics and Dangerous Drugs and now DEA) Agent, Ron Wentz.

Elvis and BNDD Agent Ron Wentz

When the troops arrived, Elvis greeted each one of them and Ron (Wentz) and I began snapping pictures.

Jerry Frazzini, Chuck Wilson, Elvis, Herb Ives, Sonny West, Jerry, Me, and Ron

Elvis and me 1970

After the photo session, Elvis went to his room and came back carrying a black brief case. Elvis was eager to open the case and display his pistols.

Elvis displaying his gun collection 1970 Radisson Hotel

It was late afternoon before the crew was ready to leave for the airport and Elvis shook our hands and expressed his appreciation for everything. He said he would be seeing us again. Elvis asked Jerry for a phone number so he could contact him.

When the group left the hotel, I was exhausted, but I couldn't have been more thrilled because it was like a daydream to have met and have photos taken with Elvis.

The Elvis visit was big news for the entire police department, then and now.

I was anxious to see the Elvis photos so my wife and I took one roll to the grocery store to be developed, while another undeveloped roll was still in my camera. After picking up the developed roll, I stupidly put the photos on top of our car when I was getting my keys. Forgetting them I drove off. When we discovered what I had done, we frantically retraced our route. We also and checked to see if someone had returned the package to the store, No such luck.

We carefully and very slowly drove back to our home using the same route taken when we left the store, looking very closely at the road hoping to find the packet of pictures. We did this several times for a couple of days, even returning to the store asking again if someone turned any pictures in. Our name, home telephone number and address were on the packet so we were hoping that someone would call us if they found them.

A call came a few days later from a man who wouldn't identify himself. He said he found the pictures in the grocery store parking lot and for a price he would return them. I would not be blackmailed and refused to pay the ransom. Sometime later my billfold, that also contained some Elvis photos, was stolen out of a gym locker near my home. I had put my contact information on the back of these photos, but they also were never returned. I sure wish back then the sophisticated tracking devices of today were available, because I would have used them to try and track down the missing photos.

After Elvis died, some of my stolen pictures appeared in magazines. When I contacted the publications no one would disclose how they got the photos.

Thankfully, I still have many other photos I took with Elvis and you can be sure I keep a close eye on them.

The hoopla from the Elvis visit eventually died down and we all went back to work with little thought of Elvis' comment that he would see us again.

Being the gentleman that Elvis was, he kept his word.

Lt. Elvis and Jerry

Chapter 2
ELVIS IN LAS VEGAS
January 31, 1971

Elvis came through with the promise he made when we met him the previous November in Denver, to call Jerry, who now had been promoted to captain. He invited Jerry, Ron and me to come to his opening concert and dinner engagement at the International Hotel (later the Hilton), in Las Vegas, also to celebrate his daughter, Lisa Marie's, third birthday.

Before the call, I really didn't believe we would ever see Elvis in person again.

Jerry, Ron and I were previously scheduled to be in Grand Canyon, Arizona on February 2, 1971, to conduct a three-day law enforcement training class at the Horace M. Albright training center.

We already had a flight booked changing airplanes in Las Vegas for our Grand Canyon commitment, so I called the training coordinator to see if after the training we could head back earlier than planned to Vegas. I told him that we had planned to meet Elvis for one of his concerts. "No problem," he said.

This was my first time in Las Vegas and I really didn't know what to expect. We flew out of Stapleton International in

Denver and arrived at the much smaller McCarran International Airport on January 31, 1971.

I had lived in communities where most shops close and sidewalks "roll-up" on Sundays. Not Las Vegas. All of the casinos were lit up like Christmas trees and it was still daylight outside. Crowds of people were bustling in and out of the casinos. Traffic cruised up and down the strip, bumper to bumper. We finally arrived at the International Hotel, 3000 Paradise Road, which I would guess from the costly taxi ride was several miles east of the airport.

International Hotel-Las Vegas 1971

I later learned from Joe Esposito that the taxi driver likely recognized us as first-time tourists and took the longer scenic ride to the hotel. It was well worth the extra miles and cost to travel the longer route and see the strip.

Elvis' penthouse suite was perched in the sky - I believe somewhere around the 30th floor. Just riding the fast elevator was like riding an amusement park ride.

Joe Esposito and Jerry, Las Vegas 1971

Elvis was napping so Jerry and I went to check out the hotel and casino.

The slot machines were back to back and lined up everywhere we walked and the players had plastic cups waiting to be filled with coins.

The noise from the slots was overwhelming for us Denverites, not used to taking in the Vegas atmosphere all at once, and Jerry wanted to find a quieter place to sit. We ended

up playing Keno, which was like playing Bingo and boring but I won my money back and got a free drink to boot.

What change I had left was burning a hole in my pocket so I decided to try my luck feeding a slot machine. It was exciting to pull the arm and watch and hear the wheel spin, but my money quickly disappeared and I moved on.

On my way to meet Jerry, the Blackjack tables called my name. I had to try one hand. I was down to one last dollar chip to "hit or stand." I folded and placed the remaining chip in my pocket for a long lasting souvenir and reminder that you can't beat the dealer. I backed away from the table and my careful eye wandered to the scantily clad women who distracted those taking part in the game by asking, "Can I get you drink, cigarette or cigar?" Their efforts won some money for the casinos when some of the players forgot to "hit or stand."

It was early evening when we met up with Elvis in his suite.

Once again, he brought out his gun collection to show us. It had grown from the small brief case, which we saw in Denver, to a larger case

Elvis made me nervous when he would take one of his guns out of the case and point it at some object as if he was preparing to shoot it. I asked Elvis if the guns were empty of bullets and he assured me they were.

I had reason to be more paranoid than the others in the room because in 1965 I shot my right big toe with a gun I thought was empty.

Elvis also proudly displayed his collection of law enforcement badges. Elvis was like a little kid wannabe cop collecting law enforcement badges. The only real difference is kids have to save up their allowances to buy toy badges at a store. Elvis wanted real badges and he generally got what he wanted because he knew who to ask.

A good example was on his acquired Federal BNDD badge and his meeting with President Nixon on December 21, 1970. When I told Elvis I would be attending the BNDD Academy he excitedly asked me all about it. I told him what it was about and promised to tell him more after I finished the training. Forgetting about BNDD, Elvis then turned to Jerry and asked him when he was going to get a Denver Police Captain's badge to replace the Lieutenant badge he got during his visit to Denver. Jerry assured him the next time he was in Denver he'd get a captain badge.

When I attended the BNDD ten-week training academy in 1971 in Washington, D.C. people there were still talking about Elvis and the efforts he went through with President Nixon to get a BNDD badge.

Our conversation with Elvis in his suite stopped when Elvis' long time manager, Colonel Parker entered. He told Elvis he was going to get some exercise.

Elvis told me: "The Colonel is heading for the casino. That's what he means by getting some exercise."

Elvis turned to me and asked if I would watch the Colonel. He also asked that I call him "EP" like his other close friends. It never felt quite right. "The Colonel has a gambling problem Bob, and I want to make sure he doesn't get carried away," Elvis explained. "He has lost a lot of money gambling."

Jerry looked and me and told Elvis, "Bob will do a great job."

Associated Press
Col. Tom Parker helped guide Elvis Presley's career.

Presley manager dies at 87

By The Associated Press

LAS VEGAS, Nev. — Col. Tom Parker, the former carnival barker who helped guide Elvis Presley to stardom, died yesterday of complications from a stroke. He was 87.

Col. Tom Parker (1909-1997)
Gazette Telegraph-Associated Press

I asked Elvis what I should do if the Colonel got out of hand. Elvis told me, "Just tap him on the shoulder and tell him to be careful." I wasn't happy about this task because we were supposed to be on vacation, but it was hard to turn down a request from Elvis.

I had met the Colonel in Denver and never felt comfortable around him. He was standoffish and acted like a "bigga shit" – as my Italian buddies would say. I also could tell that the Colonel didn't care for the posse that Elvis had around him

The Colonel wasn't hard to spot when I exited the elevator. He wore a hat, similar to a cowboy hat but smaller and he was chomping on a big cigar. When he passed by slot machines he wouldn't sit down, but would just stand and drop coins into the machines, pulling the arm and watching the wheel spin. Often I could hear "ding-ding" as coins he won hit the metal catch. He eventually moved to the Roulette table.

I stood a short distance behind him and it was obvious he had been at this particular Roulette table before by the way he was greeted. The Colonel would lay a lot of money down buying chips. He placed bets on the numbers. He was losing "big time." You would think that he knew, what I knew from studying gambling, that Roulette odds are the worst in a casino.

It was getting close to the time Elvis would perform and I didn't want to miss the show. When I moved in closer to the Colonel and violated his space, he looked up at me with an angry glare. The Colonel recognized me from being around Elvis, and to say the Colonel was mad would be an understatement. I was surprised how loud he was when he told me, "Elvis always wants someone watching me, and someone should be watching Elvis' elaborate spending."

Everyone at the table stopped and paid more attention to us than where the wheel was going to stop. The Colonel got up from the Roulette table, collected his money and we both went to the elevator. I thought about waiting for another elevator, but I told Elvis I would watch him and didn't want him ditching me by getting off at a different floor

Neither of us spoke during the elevator ride. When the doors opened, the Colonel made a beeline to Elvis and they disappeared into Elvis' bedroom. I stayed with Jerry and told him what had happened.

When Elvis and Colonel came out, Elvis was smiling and the Colonel was fuming as he made a dash out of the suite.

Elvis said, "Thanks Bob, the Colonel is obsessed with gambling. You kept him from losing big." I turned to Jerry and softly said, "I don't think so Jerry, I saw him put some big wads of money down."

Elvis told us some unexpected news when he shared that there had been threats made on his life. The FBI and local police – along with his bodyguards – were on high alert. He added that he wasn't scared - placing his hand on a small revolver he had stuck in his belt, guaranteeing me that this gun was "loaded."

Similar to the Denver concert, Elvis was in his signature jump suit: women went crazy screaming and his bodyguards kept everyone at a distance. As law enforcement officers, we were also on high alert because of the death threat but the concert was great and went without incident.

Ron, Joe, me and G. Starkey in Las Vegas

After the concert, Jerry, Ron and I went up to Elvis's suite and celebrated his daughter's birthday with a large group of people. Ron told me Priscilla Presley was present, but I didn't see her. I didn't mix with the crowd and preferred to stay in the shadows. After the birthday party, the majority of the guests went down to the dance floor that was part of Elvis' suite. Jerry and Ron decided to go to the casino but it was way past midnight and I told them I was going to bed.

Before taking my leave, I noticed a staircase leading down from Elvis' suite to where people were dancing and talking. I decided to watch for a while and took a seat toward the top. It wasn't long before Elvis shocked me and joined me on the stairs.

Elvis had a cigarillo that had a plastic tip, in his mouth. I never did see him light it. I asked if I could see one of the cigars. He took small packet from his shirt pocket. The cigar was a Villiger Kiel.

Villiger Kiel Cigars **Courtesy of Anne Dinkins**
Customer Service/Procurement

I will never forget because I wrote it down. When I got back to Denver I went to a cigar specialty store downtown to purchase some. They were a lot more expensive than the usual Roitan's I carried and could be found at any store.

Elvis wanted to pick up our conversation about my attending the BNDD Academy and probed me more about it. I explained it was a training academy for local law enforcement officers from all over the U.S. and other countries. The school was ten weeks long and the training is abbreviated from what BNDD agents go through. The expectations were to train us to go back to our states and team up with BNDD agents to fight drug trafficking.

He was very attentive. I didn't have all the answers for him but assured him again that I would let him know the next time we saw each other.

Elvis looked strangely at me and asked if I was okay. I told him, "EP I am great. I sure didn't mean to make the Colonel mad." Elvis said, "I have been meaning to tell you Bob, again, thanks. This is good the Colonel knows I am keeping an eye on his gambling habit."

I changed the subject telling Elvis I always liked watching people and studying their movements. Their behavior can tell you a lot of what's going on. Whenever I need to go to the airport, I get there early just to watch the people. I even once made a drug bust watching a guy, and missed my flight.

Elvis asked if I had studied him.

I said, "Yes Elvis. I have noticed your actions are different according to who you are with."

Since he asked, I told him the truth. He didn't seem happy with my honesty.

There was a case of mineral water on a table next to the staircase that was close to where we were sitting and Elvis asked me to grab him a bottle. I knew from when he was in Denver that Elvis had Mountain Valley Spring Water with him from Tennessee when he traveled

I told him I didn't mind fetching his water but jokingly added I wasn't his valet. He gave me a look and I thought, "Oh shit, what did I just say; joking or not, here I go again, speaking before thinking."

Elvis continued to stare at me while my mind started spinning: How do I get out of this? I thought I would try to humor him and said, "EP, when you get up in the morning do you pee and put your pants on the same as I do?"

He answered, "yes" to my question but didn't laugh or grin. When I went to get the water Elvis grabbed my arm and told me to sit down, that he would get the water himself. While I was hoping Jerry would appear and get me out of this mess I also thought some more humor might help.

While I held my breath, he picked up a bottle and gave it to me. All I could say was, "Thanks EP," and pray he didn't tell Jerry about the exchange.

But he actually seemed to relax and he sat down for more "small talk." This was the only time he ever mentioned the use of drugs to me. He said he slept during the day to reserve his energy for the concerts but then it took him a long time to wind down before he could sleep and often needed sleep aids.

Courtesy John Porter Director of Ecommerce
Mountain Valley Spring Company

If he had taken anything before he sat down next to me or when he left, he sure didn't show any signs.

The rest of our talk was about his mother and his life. He told me that his dad was in jail, that they had to move several times, and the bank repossessed his dad's car. He also said his dad had been fired from jobs.

I said Elvis "Are you sure Elvis you are not talking about me?" I had a similar upbringing as you did, and we were dirt poor. My dad couldn't keep a job because of his drug addiction. I went to five high schools and lived with various relatives."

Elvis looked at me and jokingly said, "Can you sing Bob?" "You got one up on me Elvis. You could be a policeman but I could never be a singer."

I was captivated just sitting there and talking with Elvis just like another friend. He asked more about my family and being a police officer, but before I could tell him more, Joe arrived and asked Elvis to come with him to meet someone.

Fueled by our discussion, I wasn't sleepy and found Jerry and Ron in the casino. We spent several hours along the strip. We visited several casinos, each one graciously accepting the money we left behind.

Before we left for the airport to travel to the Grand Canyon, Elvis gave us each a TCB (Taking Care of Business) fourteen-karat gold necklace. He said he gave similar necklaces only to his very close friends. This was a sign we were in his inner circle.

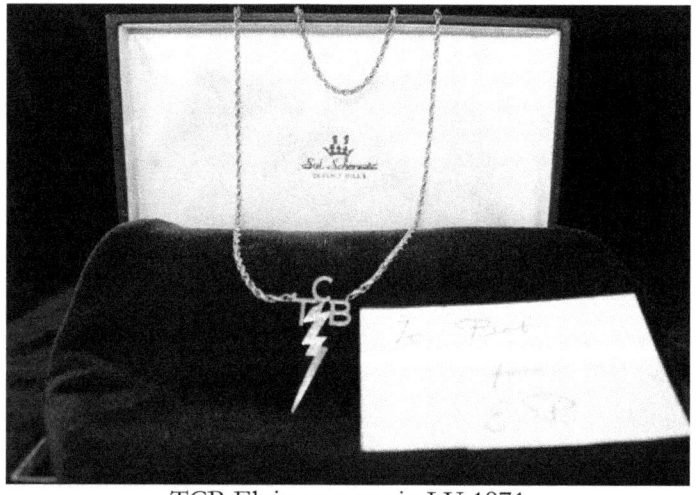

TCB Elvis gave me in LV 1971

Jeweler Sol Schwartz of Beverly Hills, California, confirmed to me that he had made the TCB necklaces for Elvis. Each TCB was in a black jewelry case and Elvis signed each one.

Mine said, "To Bob from EP." I felt extremely privileged that Elvis gave me a TCB.

My first meeting with Elvis in Denver didn't get off to a good start and the Colonel's anger here in Vegas made me feel like I had been screwing up. The rocky conversation on the staircase also had me worried until toward the end when he shared his stories. The necklace confirmed my thought that Elvis really wanted to be treated like an equal instead of a superstar.

I was surprised to get the necklace, and was surprised again when Elvis said he wanted to fly our wives to Vegas to meet us when we returned from our training session. Wow!

This curve ball left me telling Elvis the women may need more time for the trip but his reply cemented that all of our wives were coming to Vegas.

Elvis said, "I want to have them attend one of my dinner shows and I will take care of all expenses. I know you guys are on tight budgets."

We fell over each other getting to the phones: so anxious to call our wives. I will never forget the call to my wife and how excited she was to get to see Elvis, his concert, Las Vegas and fly on a plane for the first time.

"Sometimes we take it for granted, since we see so many entertainers and dignitaries while our wives take care of the home front and only hear our stories," I told Elvis. "Now they will have stories to tell."

After the training at the Grand Canyon, we headed back to Vegas where we met our wives at the airport and showed them the strip on the way to our hotel.

Me at Grand Canyon 1971

If Elvis had not funded this trip for my wife, this once in a lifetime opportunity for her would never have happened. More thrills came when she met Elvis and we had VIP treatment at the dinner show.

As we were waiting in line to get into the showroom, a concierge staff came up and asked if we were Elvis' guests from Colorado.

I was more than ecstatic to say, "Yes!" Feeling very important but remaining unassuming, we all followed the concierge bypassing the long line. The first thing my wife saw was the enormous beautiful room with tables and booths everywhere. Bragging, I told her I had seen it before.

The concierge led us to seats right in front of the stage. We were so close that my wife actually placed her hand on the stage.

Back row: Gerald and Angela Starkey, Joan and Jerry Kennedy. Front from the back: Gene and Betty Kennedy, Gloria and Herb Ives, and me and Jody. Elvis dinner show Las Vegas 1971

Once the drum roll began to play and Elvis entered the stage we knew it was going to be a night filled with many forever memories. After singing a song or two Elvis requested the house lights be shown on our table. As the lights moved our way he began telling the audience he had some special Denver Police friends and their wives with us tonight. It was strange to hear the crowd applaud us and even better when the hotel gave us champagne glasses to commemorate the event.

During the concert he sang some special songs for us, including "Sweet Caroline" for my wife. To this day she gets excited when she hears it.

After the show, Elvis graciously invited all of us to his suite for glasses of champagne and photos with our wives. Elvis gave our wives many great memories that night and for years to come.

Elvis and my wife Jody, Las Vegas 1971

Elvis and Jerry's wife Joan in Las Vegas 1971

Dr. Starkey picking his wife up at Las Vegas airport 1971

Dee and Vernon Presley in Las Vegas

I made sure to guard this undeveloped film.

The next day we were headed back to the airport to return to Denver. While we were waiting, Ron was the first one to spot Priscilla Presley. She was very striking and stood out in the crowd of travelers. Unfortunately, our flight was boarding and we had no time to talk with her.

That was the only disappointment of the trip.

Chapter 3
ELVIS DONATES $5,000
DENVER POLICE GYM FUND
October 1971

NADING-PRESLEY MEMORIAL GYM

ON OCTOBER 3, 1971, DENVER POLICE OFFICER MERLE NADING WAS SLAIN BY A GUNMAN AT COLFAX AVENUE AND GAYLORD STREET. OFFICER NADING WAS WELL RESPECTED BY HIS FELLOW OFFICERS AND HIS PASSING WAS A BLOW FELT BY ALL. AT THE TIME OF HIS DEATH, OFFICER NADING HAD BEGUN WORK ON THIS GYM, AND AS A TRIBUTE TO HIM HIS FELLOW OFFICERS HAVE COMPLETED IT WITH THEIR OWN UNSELFISH WORK.
THE THOUSANDS OF DOLLARS USED TO PURCHASE MATERIALS FOR THIS GYM WERE DONATED BY ELVIS PRESLEY, WHO CONTRIBUTED THE MONEY TO THE DENVER POLICE DEPARTMENT FOR THIS PURPOSE.
THE NADING-PRESLEY MEMORIAL GYM STANDS AS A MEMORIAL TO BOTH OF THESE FINE MEN AND ALL OTHERS WHO CONTRIBUTED TIME AND EFFORT TO ITS SUCCESSFUL COMPLETION.

After our Vegas visit, Elvis made spur of the moment stops in Denver. One such visit happened in October 1971, when the Denver Police Department was mourning the murder of DPD patrolman Merle Nading.

Elvis arrived during the manhunt for the suspect who killed our colleague.

Officer Nading was stationed at DPD substation District 2, at 3555 Colorado Blvd., in northeast Denver.

DPD Officer Merle Nading (courtesy DPD)

The area he patrolled included East Colfax Avenue and Gaylord Street, just east of downtown Denver.

On Sunday, October 3, 1971, he was attempting to quiet a disturbance between a man and a woman quarreling in the parking lot of Clark's Diner at 2201 East Colfax Ave. Officer Nading arrested the man on a disturbance charge.

Patrons of a nearby bar gathered in the parking lot and started harassing Officer Nading. An off-duty officer came to the aid of Nading and took custody of the suspect while Nading went back to his patrol car to inform the dispatcher that an unruly crowd was growing. One man in the crowd threw a punch at Nading and when he started to arrest the man another male interfered. Nading grabbed the other man and held him around the neck. During the struggle, the man reached around Officer Nading and grabbed the officer's gun and fired, fatally shooting Nading in the back. Hearing the shot, the crowd quickly dispersed and fled the parking lot, including the shooter.

The suspect was eventually caught and charged with Nading's murder but he was acquitted at trial.

Jerry told me Elvis was visibly shaken when he heard about the ruthless killing of officer Nading and he wanted to do something. Kennedy told Elvis that before his untimely death Nading had started work to remodel the gym in the basement of the District 2 station.

Elvis unselfishly wrote a check for $5,000 to the Denver Police Department for the completion of the District 2 gym. The money helped turn the plain concrete walls in the basement into a finished room with updated equipment.

DPD Captain Tina Lewis Rowe, recalled being summoned to the chief's office for a photo with Elvis, when he was there presenting the check for the Nading Memorial Gym. She said, "I only had about two years on the job, so I made a remark about feeling embarrassed at being in the chief's office. Elvis was very gracious and said, 'Let me get a nice photo with you, Honey.' After the photographer took our picture, Elvis said, 'Why don't you take one that's more friendly?' He leaned toward me and gave me what I considered to be a very sweet feeling kiss! I was completely surprised and when it ended—all of two seconds later—I blurted, 'If you're lucky, I'll give you my autograph.' He smiled a bit and chuckled. I was ushered out the door and my moment was over. I look at that photo now and see me in my homemade dress with an embarrassed smile and I cringe. But, the memory of being kissed by Elvis makes up for it!"

Elvis and Tina Rowe 1971

Elvis didn't ask for any recognition but the department did not want his contribution to go unnoticed. They named the renovated area, which opened October 7, 1972, the Nading-Presley Memorial Gym and included Presley's contribution on a bronze dedication plaque.

The plaque reads in part: "Officer Nading was well respected by his fellow officers and his passing was a blow felt by all. The Nading-Presley Memorial Gym stands as a memorial to both of these fine men and all others who contributed time and effort to its successful completion."

The Denver Police Department has since relocated District 2 to a new station house at 3921 Holly Street and Elvis' generosity won't be forgotten because the plaque also was moved to the new station.

Every time he visited the Mile High City, Elvis left a positive mark on individuals and in this case the entire DPD community and beyond.

Chapter 4
ELVIS CONCERT IN DENVER
April 30, 1973

Elvis autographed to Ron and me

Elvis performed back-to-back concerts in other cities before coming to Denver on April 30, 1973 for his third concert at the Denver Coliseum.

Elvis looked exhausted when he arrived several hours before the show. Jerry, Ron and I were outfitted in our DPD uniforms, ready to work off-duty at the concert when we greeted him. He embraced me and shook my hand before asking about my family.

I leaned over and quietly told Jerry I was concerned about how Elvis looked. "I feel bad for Elvis, he seems worn out. Is the money worth his health?"

Jerry whispered he wasn't sure what was wrong but his road manager said Elvis' schedule was packed.

I walked over to where Elvis and Ron were talking and asked Elvis if he was OK. He thanked me for the concern and said the tour had been draining but he'd be ready for the concert after a rest. I slapped him on the back and told him we'd see him at the concert.

The concert was sold out and fans were arriving early and the line outside the Coliseum continued to grow.

Jerry designated me the officer in charge of the other off-duty police working the event. "You know your job," Jerry said. "Keep the crowd orderly and from crashing the gates."

It was cold and lightly raining. The temperature continued to dip. Most of the women waiting in line weren't dressed for the changing spring weather, typical of Colorado. I actually felt sorry for them. I went inside and found the Coliseum director. He agreed to open the gates earlier than planned because of the cold weather.

When the gates opened, the crowd roared their appreciation. The other officers and I were very appreciative also.

Once the doors opened the ticket-takers hurriedly inspected each ticket to ensure they weren't counterfeit and ushered the people in quickly through the gates (lined by rails on each side). I was amazed; there was no stampede, excessive pushing or crowding and the ushers quickly directed them to their assigned seating.

When the jam-packed entrance began to clear, a couple of officers remained inside close to the gates, meanwhile   the other officers and I tried to keep the fans from blocking the corridor so others could get to their seats. The souvenir vendors that were selling all sorts of Elvis paraphernalia from their booths that lined the corridor were causing part of the congestion.

When it came time for Elvis to arrive at the Coliseum I met up with Jerry at the rear entrance. Ron had stayed at the hotel and came with Elvis and his entourage to the Coliseum. Ron made certain the off-duty officers securing the Coliseum's VIP parking area ushered their cars in. Elvis was then escorted through the back entrance, which was also being safeguarded by two off-duty officers.

Jerry and I guided Elvis and the others to an area reserved for his dressing room.

I was relieved to see that, in the short time since Elvis arrived in Denver, he transformed from the exhausted man we originally saw to the Elvis I knew when we first met.

He was in good form, laughing and having a bit of fun with us.

While Elvis was getting ready to go on stage, some fans tried to get a close-up glance of "The King" but they couldn't get past his bodyguards, or Jerry, Ron and me.

Comic Jackie Kahane—was the opening act and after intermission Elvis got ready to take the stage in his signature white jumpsuit and jewelry. At that time I noticed something. Elvis must dye his hair before his shows. His jumpsuit with a high white collar accented his now jet-black hair.

While age was creeping up on all of us, we still visited like a bunch of schoolboys while Elvis waited to take the stage.

Joe gave the hand sign to the orchestra and they hammered out the theme from "2001: A Space Odyssey". Elvis twisted his neck to relieve stress, took a couple of deep breaths, shook his hands and was ready. The fans went nuts.

What fun it was to be standing by The King once again and I was even being paid to be there. I knew many people who would die for the chance just to see the concert, let alone be this close to the legend.

Several officers lined up in front of the stage to keep fans from jumping on to the stage. When Elvis took the stage the arena exploded with screaming Elvis devotees and flashing light bulbs from their cameras. Crowds of women jumped from their seats and ran to the stage screaming "Elvis! Elvis!" We had our hands full.

Keeping the fans from getting up on the stage that night was a harder task than what we encountered at the Radisson in 1970, when we kept the screaming women from getting off the elevator. While we kept the fans off the stage, several pitched flowers and other gifts over us and on to the stage.

You would never know that Elvis performed the night before in Seattle, Washington. He was full of vim and vigor and ready to perform.

"Thank you, ladies and gentlemen. Thank you very much;" Elvis was in full swing pounding out some of his earlier and recent songs. There was some pushing and shoving close to the stage, but no one was hurt and very respectful of officer commands to settle down.

Like the 1970 concert in Denver, the women went nuts when he used his scarves to wipe the sweat from his brow and gave a few of them to the women at the front. He also threw some towards the women who couldn't manage to get close to the stage. He leaned down to get a few pecks on the cheek from the women near the stage and he kissed a few cheeks in return.

I didn't get to visit with Elvis that much this time but the concert reminded me how his fans adored him. When it was announced after the concert that "ELVIS HAS LEFT THE BUILDING" there was a mad rush for us to get him and his entire entourage out of the building before fans discovered what door he was exiting.

His grueling schedule meant he went right from this concert to the airport to board his private plane and fly to Lake Tahoe, Nevada for another concert. Jerry and Ron made the trip with Elvis, but I had to pass.

While more screaming women would greet Elvis in Lake Tahoe, I was at a law enforcement training school and studying for the DPD sergeant promotional test. Time was marching on for both of us.

Chapter 5
ELVIS' GUEST AT GRACELAND
November 1973

Graceland 1973

A month after Elvis' concert in Denver, he encouraged Jerry, Ron and me to come to Graceland for a day or two. We didn't hesitate to accept the invitation. I had seen Graceland once before, from outside the gates long before meeting Elvis.

Elvis sent a driver to pick us up at the Memphis Airport. I had found an old Memphis street map from when I last visited the city and I brought it along to show I knew how to get to Graceland.

I showed the driver and Ron my map that marked Graceland on Highway 51. The driver explained the city had changed the name to Elvis Presley Boulevard to acknowledge the city's most famous resident and make it easier for visitors to locate Graceland.

After some harassment from Jerry, I admitted, "Okay, my map is outdated and I will get a new map." I did before we returned to Denver.

When we arrived at the famous "Music Gates" outside of Elvis' home at 3764 Elvis Presley Boulevard we were greeted by the sentry who introduced himself as Vester Presley. He told us he was Elvis' uncle and emphasized that he was Elvis' father, Vernon's, older brother. After exchanging some pleasantries he said he was expecting us. He knew the driver and car, but he still carefully glanced over the inside of the car as he talked.

As we started the ride up the tree-lined curving lane to Graceland the variety of trees made me feel like I was in a tree nursery. It was winter and the trees were mostly naked. I told Jerry that I would sure like a chance to see Graceland in the spring or summer when the trees were full of blossoms. I had no clue then that I would see those trees again in 1976 and under the worst circumstances in 1977.

Trees at Graceland 1977

Throughout our visit, Elvis didn't venture to the front gate during the day and remained secluded in his house most of the time. When he did go outside, it was to the rear of the estate where he liked to lean on the fence and talk about his horses. Ron, who was a horse enthusiast, was able to talk to Elvis about the breed of the horses. Jerry and I were more impressed with the manicured grounds and watching the horses roam.

Since Elvis was not an early riser and I am, I relished strolling around Graceland's acres snapping photographs. I knew I could find Uncle Vester manning his post at the front entrance so I strolled over to chat with him. He was welcoming and preferred to be called Uncle Vester instead of Mr. Presley.

Uncle Vester (now) told me he was Graceland's gatekeeper and he frequently helped the grounds crew maintain Graceland's acres. While some may think it was odd to have a close family member perform Uncle Vester's responsibilities, he was very contented.

I was very impressed how Uncle Vester patiently listened to questions from visitors that steadily gathered outside of the gate. They wanted to know everything about Elvis and he took the time to answer the questions he could. He was a very proud man.

During our stay I also met Elvis' cousin Billy Smith, but he wasn't as friendly as Uncle Vester.

When I met Elvis' grandma, who wanted to be called Minnie, and his Aunt Delta, they were sitting in chairs close to where they roomed, which was close to the kitchen area. Neither one spoke much, except to each other, preferring to be nonexistent from Elvis' visitors. When I introduced myself to them, they were both very nice. For once, I didn't ask questions, respecting their privacy.

I did have one short exchange with Grandma Minnie when I was in the kitchen at the counter visiting with Elvis' cook, Mary Jenkins. Grandma came in for a glass of Mountain Valley Spring water and I asked her if I could bother her for one. She said politely, "Yes sir," and boy did that make me feel old. Then I remembered, in the South everyone says yes sir, no sir, and yes ma'am and no ma'am, regardless of their age, or yours. Elvis noticeably did also.

Courtesy John Porter Director of Ecommerce
Mountain Valley Spring Company

Eating the meals prepared by Elvis' cooks, Mary Jenkins and Pauline Nicholson, reminded me of the down-home country cooking my grandma in Texas prepared and it was down-out good.

An unexpected-surprise came while I was once again sitting at the kitchen counter visiting with Pauline and eating her recently cooked biscuits that smelled like heaven. Elvis came up behind me and put his hand on my shoulder. I got up and ask Elvis if I was in his "spot." He said no and for me to continue eating.

"My wife makes great biscuits but these are the greatest," I told Elvis, between bites.

Elvis reached over me and picked up the kitchen telephone that was attached to the wall. He asked me if my wife was home. I told him she likely was. I mentioned her name, just in case he'd forgotten from when he met her in Las Vegas.

He got the hint because when my wife answered the phone, he said, "Hello Jody."

Elvis was soon carrying on a pleasant conversation with my wife. Shortly Elvis told Jody that he was going to put his cook, Mrs. Pauline, on the phone to tell her how she makes biscuits.

I always carried a note pad and pen with me and hurriedly wrote what I could understand. My wife and Mrs. Pauline spoke the same cookery language and my wife captured the ingredients and preparation; which was a pinch of this, and a cup of that, etc.

Elvis Biscuits notes -Graceland 1973

My wife now makes impressively large biscuits she appropriately named, "Elvis' Biscuits."

With all the good meals, I needed some exercise and Elvis introduced me to racquetball at Memphis State College. To avoid any crowds around Elvis, the college opened the racquetball court in the early morning for Elvis and Dr. 'Nick' (Nichopoulas), his personal physician. Jerry and Ron had played racquetball before but I was a rookie at this sport.

I gave it my best for part of a match but I finally told Elvis it wasn't a game for my short stocky body and they all got a good laugh at my expense.

I tried to watch them play but I kept dozing off. Changing to Elvis' late-night schedule was brutal on me.

When we got back to Graceland, Elvis told us he had some information on some drug dealers in the county and was going to call Shelby County Sheriff. Elvis had told us many times that he was totally against drug dealers and that the users were victims of these predators. I assuredly agreed with him.

It was evening when the Sheriff and couple of his deputies arrived at Graceland. You could tell by the way Elvis and the Sheriff greeted each other that they had met many times before. Elvis introduced Jerry, Ron and me to the Sheriff and the deputies who were real southern gentleman. They asked us about our positions on DPD and then we talked about their work.

Finally, Elvis told the Sheriff that he had heard of some drug dealers living outside of Memphis. The two deputies took notes on the details Elvis gave them. From my experience as a 'narc,' the information was very vague and would be good intelligence, but not enough for any immediate action. A lot of follow-up would be needed. Whether the Sheriff was able to follow-up I never knew, nor did I ask Elvis.

That trip reinforced my thoughts that Elvis was very different when he was a 'free-man' to wander, without his entourage tagging along with him. He was really down to earth and a humble man that was easy to talk with.

When we visited, I didn't focus on his concerts or music but asked more about Graceland and his youth, which he enjoyed discussing. We both came from similar backgrounds so we understood some of the real hardships of having a tough childhood. We both were very proud that we were able to rise above it and have great lives for our families and ourselves.

I was able to get a glimpse into Elvis' private life and our visit ended when he told us he was leaving Graceland for another trip. I respected his hospitality and privacy and didn't need to say much more than "thank you Elvis, I had a great time and hope I to see you again." Jerry and Ron echoed the same appreciation.

We left Graceland, wishing we could have stayed longer, but Elvis was leaving Graceland. I didn't ask him where or why.

Chapter 6
ELVIS VACATIONS IN VAIL
January 7-January 20, 1976

**Elvis waiting at motel (1976) to travel to Vail
with his DPD Captains badge on**

I was unpacking from a trip to New York City where, I was working–a major Denver Organized Crime murder case, with DPD Detective Joel Humphrey, that involved two NYPD officers, when I got a call from Jerry on Tuesday, January 6, 1976.

Jerry asked me if I could get some time off and stay with Elvis in Vail where he planned to vacation and celebrate his 41st birthday. Jerry said Elvis initially wanted to go to Aspen after he saw on TV some people skiing there. But Jerry suggested

Vail instead, because it was closer to Denver, less crowded than Aspen and he'd have more options for lodging. Jerry also asked if I would be available, with Ron, to pick up Joe from the airport early Wednesday morning.

Although, I was the Project Coordinator for the Colorado Organized Crime Strike Force (OCSF), I felt I needed to run it by the OCSF Project Director, because Ron and I had several on-going investigations. I assured the Director that I would stay in frequent contact with him and be readily available if we needed to return to Denver. He OK'd the trip.

When we picked up Joe at the airport he told us he was still working to get lodging in Vail. Meanwhile, Elvis and his crew would stay at the Ramada Inn, 4735 Kipling Street, in the West Denver suburb of Wheat Ridge. It made sense to stay there because once they were ready to head to Vail they would get on nearby Interstate 70 and head due west to Vail.

Ramada Inn (now American Inn)

Jerry was already at the motel when we arrived.

Finding a place in Vail was a challenge. Ron and Jerry had some contacts and lined up a couple of places for Joe to look at. While we were sitting in the motel discussing it, Elvis and his entourage unexpectedly showed up earlier than Joe expected. Joe turned to us and said, "Just like Elvis, he is unpredictable, and when he gets anxious on the spur of the moment, his plans and ours change."

Arriving with Elvis was his girlfriend, Linda Thompson, along with the wives and girlfriends of the other guys. Even though we were still a two-hour drive from the ski slopes, they all were dressed in ski gear.

Elvis was the same, as always, shaking our hands and embracing each of us with a big Southerly hug.

Joe was exhausted and said he was looking forward to crashing in his room and meeting up with Elvis the next day. But Ron told Joe he could rest in the car while driving the 100 miles to Vail. Jerry and I stayed with Elvis.

Courtesy Vail Visiting Center

Jerry had invited now Denver Police Chief Art Dill to meet Elvis and Elvis was delighted when the Chief arrived.

Watching their conversation was entertaining because it was like a contest of who could tell the most stories and jokes. Jerry also added a few "off-color" comments that made both men laugh.

DPD Chief Art Dill, Elvis and Jerry

Then Jerry got serious and presented Elvis with a Kel-Lite flashlight for his birthday. He knew Elvis would like it because the flashlight is the type carried by police officers, because it is a durable and bright light, and it was something he could use while in Vail.

Chief Dill told Elvis "Happy Birthday" and presented him a gold DPD Captain's badge and pinned it on Elvis' ski parka. Elvis was pleased with both gifts and became emotional.

His reaction made me think how much he appreciated unexpected gifts with no-strings, unlike the people on his payroll that felt obligated to give him gifts. The moment gave me chills. Incidentally, Elvis did not remove his new captain's badge from his ski parka the entire time he was in Vail.

Next, it was time for Elvis to show us his growing handgun collection.

Elvis knew every gun he had and where and when he purchased it or who gave him one. Elvis took a gun out of the case and presented it to Chief Dill and then another to Jerry. I was busy taking photographs so maybe that's why Elvis didn't give me a gun. He also knew from our time together in Vegas that I wasn't a gun enthusiast.

Instead, Elvis asked me to be part of a karate demonstration put on by his karate trainer that he had brought on the trip. Elvis assured me the karate moves wouldn't hurt. It did hurt.

"If he hits me again, I'll show him my street karate," I said loud enough for everyone to hear.

Chief Dill told me I'd been hit harder in other circumstances and to calm down.

"Calm down hell!" I said louder, lifting my shirt and showing the red welts on my chest. Elvis started to laugh then stopped the demonstration.

I was told later that Elvis got fed up with the instructor and dropped him from his traveling crew.

The next day, Ron and Joe booked Vella Cortina and the Deauville House located on the east end of Vail known as the Golden Peak area. Both houses backed up to Vail Ski Area and groomed slopes.

Where we stayed in Vail 1976

Elvis wanted to leave right away for Vail, but Jerry told him we didn't have enough vehicles for everyone. Elvis' solution; get a Trailways bus, and Jerry did.

I told Elvis I couldn't leave with them because I had another obligation the following day.

"Cancel it and come with us Bob." Elvis said.

"Elvis I can't, as much as I would like to, but I am scheduled to be at the police academy tomorrow morning." I said.

I waited for Chief Dill to give me an excused absence from the academy but that didn't happen, perhaps because the chief also couldn't make the bus ride.

"That's a first," Elvis said. "When I ask someone to go with me they usually jump at it."

Jerry told me Elvis spoke about the exchange all the way to Vail.

I waited until everyone was on the bus and traveling toward the snow-covered mountains before I left.

After my work at the academy the next day, I drove up to Vail and arrived by early evening.

Jerry updated me on the bus trip. They sang Christmas carols during the ride and when they arrived it was already dark, and the ski slopes were lit up. He rubbed it in that they all had a good time.

"I feel bad enough already Jerry," I told him.

I learned more details of the two places where we stayed from Dr. Donald Huttner who owned the Vella Cortina. He said he had rented it to Elvis for about $1,000 a day.

The employees at both houses were very nice and I was surprised in 1977 when a housekeeper who worked at the Deaville House, told the Rocky Mountain News that Presley was the only person that stayed there who failed to tip her at the end of the vacation.

This was unlike Elvis, who lavishly gave money or gifts to strangers. I can only presume, knowing Elvis, this was to be taken care of by one of his entourage. If Elvis had heard of this I have no doubt he would have made it more than right with the housekeeper.

We all had to get back on Elvis' time schedule of being up and entertained into the wee morning hours. One day he wanted to go snowmobiling and instead of renting a few, he bought at least three snowmobiles and other ski accessories, He bought a pair of snow boots for me since I had none with me, nor did I own a pair. After the trip, the snowmobiles were left with Ron for future use by Elvis.

Snow Boots Elvis Bought for me in Vail

Elvis was a sight to be seen. He wore a black facemask, had a cigar protruding from the mask and a pistol stuck in his pants. When I was with Elvis on the slopes he asked if he could have one of my cigars, since he had left his in the Condo. I gave him one of mine, a Roitan, a cheap cigar compared to his Villiger Kiel cigarillos. Elvis was not a chain-smoker but an edgy-smoker leaving partially burnt cigarillos in the ashtrays.

Snowmobiling with Elvis meant there were no rules governing usage of the ski area. That meant driving snowmobiles over the mounds of snow on the well-groomed slopes. It was dark, very early in the morning on Elvis' time and no skiers were on the slopes, so we had great fun jumping these mounds in the snowmobiles. However, one of his guests got hurt. Elvis' personal physician, Dr. Nick Nichopoulos' son, Dean, badly sprained his knee when he came down a slope on a snowmobile.

Jerry and Elvis, still wearing his ski mask, took him to the hospital in Vail while Ron and I stayed at the condo.

When Jerry got back he said, "People at the hospital asked the "mask-man" who he was and Elvis said 'the Lone Ranger.' "

Vail is a small town – even smaller in 1976 - so almost everyone was aware Elvis was vacationing there.

The ski area put up with our snowmobiling for a few days but then Vail police officers told us to stop driving over the moguls. It can take hours with heavy machinery to shape the mounds of snow and we certainly weren't helping their efforts.

The officers recognized Elvis with his black ski mask and it didn't change their minds about asking us to keep off the slopes.

Jerry apologized for all of us and we soon left the area.

Even though I am a Colorado native, this was the first time I had been snowmobiling, skiing or even heard the term "moguls."

I told Elvis that the ski area should have a slope for just snowmobiling. He agreed and didn't seem concerned, and said, "Bob, we sure had fun didn't we?" I excitingly said, "We sure did."

The activities wore us out and Jerry, Ron and I found secluded spots in the condo to relax when we could.

When Elvis moved around everyone better be ready. He found me resting on a couch and asked where Jerry was. I went looking and found Jerry sunbathing on a cot by the swimming pool. After telling Elvis this we both walked over to the pool where Elvis started laughing and he yelled "Jerry get up."

It was a good thing Elvis wanted to find Jerry: Jerry's Irish skin would have been burnt to a crisp had we not gotten him up

The snowmobiles weren't Elvis' only purchase on the trip. He bought a total of 10 cars before he left Colorado.

Jerry told me how the car deal went down. "Elvis asked me what kind of car I was driving. I told him an Audi Fox, and Elvis told me he was going to buy me a Lincoln. I said, "No you're not." Elvis said he was and wanted me to have a Lincoln just like the one he owned."

Ron walked in and Elvis said he was going to buy Ron a Lincoln. Ron told Elvis he would rather have a Cadillac and Elvis agreed. Elvis offered to buy Dr. Starkey (Dr. Gerald Starkey, a Denver police doctor who treated a bad rash on Elvis' face from the wool ski mask) a Lincoln, too.

Elvis wanted to buy a car for Chief Dill but he refused and Elvis didn't argue."

There was no car dealership in Vail so Jerry and Ron drove Elvis back to Denver to the Kumpf Lincoln-Mercury dealership in Denver. Elvis changed his mind and wanted to buy a Rolls Royce for Jerry, who balked. Joe intervened telling Elvis, "Hey Elvis, you had one and never liked it." Elvis agreed and purchased Lincolns for Jerry and Dr. Starkey.

I met up with Elvis, Jerry, Ron and a couple of Elvis' bodyguards in Denver before heading back to Vail. Elvis was hungry so Ron suggested we eat at his friend's Italian restaurant, La Travea, in the nearby suburb of Arvada.

Elvis devoured his meal. I had never seen Elvis eat like this before and asked if he had eaten Italian food before, "Yea, but this is the best," he said.

Elvis stood up from the table and the next thing you know, he went into the kitchen and starting making pizza with the cook. It was great to see that he was having a good time and not stressed out. I told Jerry, "Elvis is normal when you leave him alone and let him do these simple things."

Back in Vail, it was late on January 15, 1976, and I was standing on the condo porch looking up at the bright clear cold sky when all of a sudden Elvis was standing next to me. He asked me what I was looking at. I told him shooting stars. All of a sudden we both watched another bright tail of a falling star flash through the cold clear sky.

Elvis put his arm around me and said, "Bob this is your lucky day. I want to give you a gift."

I told him a gift wasn't necessary because I was just grateful to spend time with him in Vail. Elvis said, "Bob you weren't up here when I told Jerry, Ron and the Doctor I was going to buy cars for them and I want you to have one."

The next day was Saturday and Red and Sonny West followed me down from Vail to my house in Arvada so I could drop off my wife's car at my house. She had been driving, "Granny," our 1954 Ford. They came inside to meet my wife and three children and were very friendly and respectful to my family. When we left, we met up with Elvis, Jerry, Ron and the others at Jack Kent Cadillac (1485 South Colorado Blvd.).

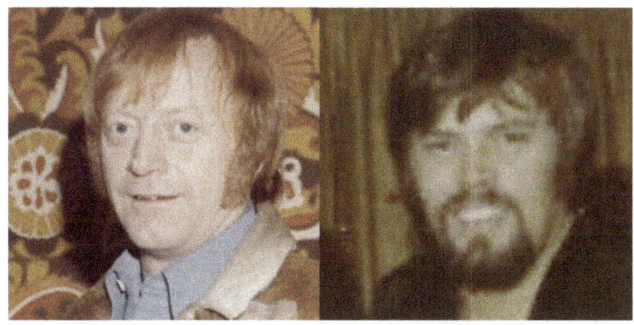

Red West   Sonny West

Later, 'Skeet' Antonio, Mr. Kent's general manager, walked me around the showroom where we viewed various 1976 Cadillac's. I picked out a yellow Cad Seville. It was the smallest of the Cad line of cars on the showroom floor and would be the least likely to draw attention from my neighbors.

Before heading back to Vail in my new shiny car, I felt it was fitting to drop by my house first, to show my family. I just couldn't wait! But then I thought about my neighbors' reactions. They saw the cars we drove and they knew I couldn't afford a Cadillac.

Jody and me with our new 1976 Cad

Our neighbors' reactions weren't on my wife's mind when she hurried down to Colorado Motor Vehicle to complete the paper work for an ELVIS specialty license plate. The ELVIS plate had already been issued so she settled for ELVISP license plate.

The excitement was exhausting. I never had dreamed of owning a new car.

One evening Elvis wanted us to give him a tour of Denver. He also wanted us to stop anyone we saw as a known crook. Thankfully, the crooks were lying low. We finally arrived back late into the night in Vail.

Once in the house, I threw myself next to Jerry and Ron on the couch, but there would be no resting that night.

Elvis brought out his numerology book. Elvis was affixed to his Cheiro's Book-of-Numbers (science of numbers) and spontaneously jumped up and said he needed and wanted, with strong emphasis on "wanted", a black diamond ring.

Elvis asked Ron if he knew a good jeweler. Ron, who had more contacts than 'Carter has Liver Pills,' said yes. But he reminded Elvis that it was Saturday and already late into the evening.

I will never forget Elvis lifting his glasses up over his eyes - like I had seen before when he really wanted to make a point - and asked Ron to work hard to contact a jeweler. Ron started making phone calls, and tracked down Denver jeweler Bob Kortz.

Kortz Jewelry was located on the 16th street mall in downtown Denver and many police officers bought jewelry there.

Thirty-six years after that unusual night, Kortz and I attended an event at Nick and Kathleen Andurlakis Café in Golden for Elvis fans. Elvis impersonator, Johnny Barber, was performing. Kortz recalled that night and his memories were reported in the Denver newspaper Westword by Mark Sanders, Dave Herrera and Steve Brown

"I had never seen a black diamond and had no clue where I could get one. But Ron said Elvis was expecting him to figure it out and Elvis had two planes waiting for the jeweler at Stapleton Airport once I located the diamond to fly me to Vail.

After a few phone calls, I finally located the gem through another local jeweler and collector of unusual stones," Kortz told Westword. "Nowadays they are made synthetically, but back then black diamonds were not so easy to track down. Tinted dark gray due to inclusions of other minerals, the diamonds are only found naturally in Brazil and the Central African Republic.

I picked up the stone and a gold ring, keeping them separate in case the King didn't like the way the two looked together. I forewent the plane and instead drove to Vail, thinking I would spend a couple days skiing anyway and watching the Super Bowl on television."

When Kortz arrived in Vail, after midnight, Ron escorted him into the room, where Elvis was eating a frozen dinner. He liked the ring and asked Kortz to have the gem set.

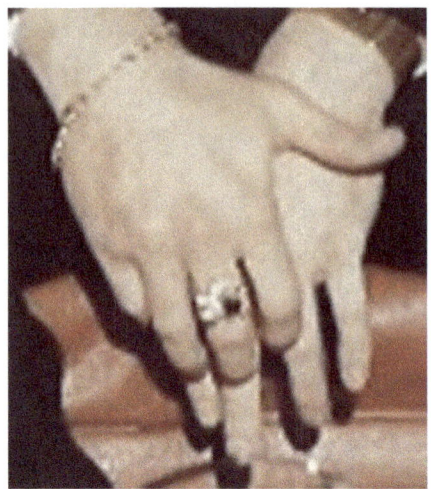

Elvis with Black Diamond Ring on 1976

Kortz said, "I made another late-night phone call to another jeweler, this time in Vail. I visited that jeweler's shop at some ungodly hour to have the stone set, and, finally, The King was satisfied."

After all of Ron's and Kortz's labors, Elvis decided he didn't like the ring and gave it to one of his entourage.

Bob Kortz

About an hour later, Elvis changed his mind and traded another piece of jewelry from his stash to get the black diamond back.

Kortz told me the ring cost about $13,000 and that he later heard the gem fell out of the setting.

Jerry told me, "The ring didn't impress me. In my opinion the black diamond was ugly and didn't look like it was worth anything, looking like black powdery 'soot', that would be hard to convince anyone it was a real diamond,"

I agreed. It looked like a black stone you can find anywhere that had been polished.

It was nearly 3 a.m. when Kortz left to go back to Denver. Elvis decided he wanted to go snowmobiling. That also meant Jerry, Ron and I were going. We donned the proper clothing and headed out into the dark early morning. Elvis wore his black facemask with a cigar protruding and pistol in his waistband.

We got little sleep after early snowmobiling but we all gathered to watch the Pittsburgh Steelers beat the Dallas Cowboys in Super Bowl X.

Two days later, while Elvis, Jerry, Ron and I were sitting on the couch talking about the great time we all had, the television was on and they were reporting Elvis' spending spree at the car dealerships.

Channel 4 Denver TV Anchor Don Kinney finished the story with a quip: "Elvis, if you're watching, I wouldn't mind an economy car."

Elvis asked Ron to call the television station, so he could talk to the newsman. When Kinney was on the phone, Ron handed it over to Elvis, who told Kinney, "You would like to have a car?"

Kinney was polite, but he didn't believe it was really Elvis. Ron called Kinney back and Kinney was certain this time; it was really Elvis.

Elvis had a new blue Cadillac Seville delivered to Kinney the following day.

The Colorado Department of Revenue would affix $13,000 for gift taxes on the cars, which Elvis paid.

Years later when I was with Joe Esposito in Kentucky, he told me that the last Cadillac Elvis bought was for him and his wife, Shirley, in 1977, not long before Elvis died.

My mistake was placing ELVISP license plates on the Cad. The media publicity caused people to stare when we were in the car.

When we parked in a shopping center or even at church we would have notes left on the windshield. They were all congratulatory but I became concerned about my wife and we decided not to drive it. We sold the car after Elvis died to Jimmy Velvet, a very good friend of Elvis' and the originator of the Elvis Presley museum that was across from Graceland.

Elvis' trip to Vail was a highlight in my life. But before he left Colorado our friendship would be tested.

Jimmy Velvet and me

Chapter 7
ELVIS UPSET WITH ME

Elvis posing at DPD

It was late afternoon on January 20, 1976; Elvis said he needed to get back to Memphis to start preparing for a recording session. Just like that the Vail excitement would be in my rear-view mirror.

I was worn out from spending time in Vail and needed rest and was anxious to get home for some of my wife's home-cooked meals; not to mention the extra jobs forewent.

As we were preparing to leave Vail for Stapleton Combs, where his private plane awaited, Joe Esposito laid some unexpected news on us; Elvis wanted some extra time to visit with Jerry, Ron and I. Joe said, "Elvis planned to stay an extra day in Denver and I made a reservation under an assumed name for him at the Stouffers Denver Inn near the airport."

I was familiar with Stouffers (changed to Clarion/Red Lion and now the Denver Doubletree Hotel, at 3203 Quebec Street) having set up a meeting with a Mexican Drug Cartel member that had flown into Denver to meet with Ron (Ron Farelli), Kenny Brown (Tony Morelli) and me (Bob Russo). Our company, Mile Hi Ski Tow Inc. was to be his drug distribution connection in Colorado; un-knowing to him we were under-cover agents with OCSF.

I was baffled why Elvis waited to tell us about the change in plans.

When we arrived at the hotel, two of his pilots were waiting in the parking lot and had his room key. With the hotel key we were able to discreetly enter the hotel through the back door that was a short distance from the elevators. Fortunately, there were no other hotel guests waiting to use the elevator.

Everything seemed to be fine. Elvis sat down and the rest of us found places to sit. Elvis appeared relaxed and asked Jerry to tell us some more humorous stories.

Elvis was holding his black and well-worn numerology book that he carried with him. I asked him if he would tell me what my wife's birthday numbers meant.

Elvis proudly and graciously did and I wrote down the gathered facts on a Stouffers' note pad that was on the desk. Then he suddenly said he wanted to rest, which didn't alarm me because he had done this before.

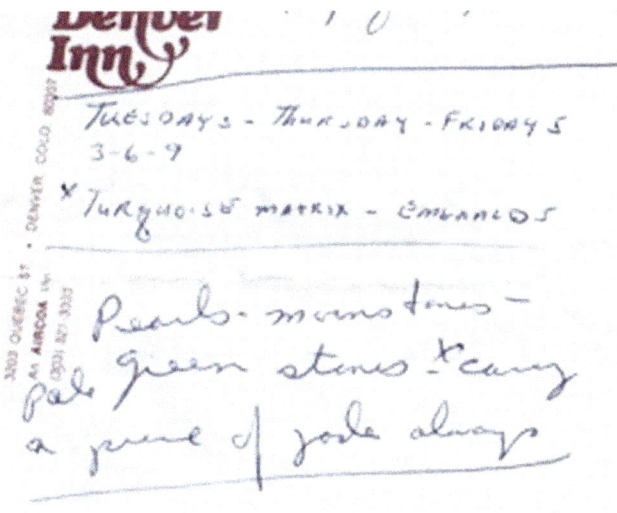

Notes I took as Elvis told me

What I had thought was going to be the reason Elvis didn't want to leave that night, was he had purchased a 10th vehicle – a pickup truck for Ron's brother, Bobby Pietrafeso, a Deputy Sheriff with the Jefferson County Sheriff's Department.

Ron had made arrangements with Jack Kent Cadillac manager 'Skeet' Antonio to pick up the truck.

Elvis was in the bedroom for just a short time before he came out and asked to speak privately with me in his room.

As I was getting up from the chair, Jerry asked me, "What does Elvis want?"

"I don't know, I have no clue, but the way he looked at me it can't be good," I said.

I followed Elvis into his bedroom. Elvis sat on the end of the bed and I remained standing in front of him.

"Bob, I hear that you have asked why I gave you a Cadillac and what did I expect from you in return," Elvis said.

He was no doubt troubled or to say the least, pissed off.

I didn't deny it and said, "Yes Elvis, no one gives you something for nothing. I learned this lesson a long time ago. I know restaurants provide food to officers for half price just to get the police to frequent their restaurants and it provides them security and patrons feel safe eating there."

I continued with other examples but Elvis interrupted: "I know Bob, but I like you guys, you treat me just like any other man, not a celebrity. The others that are always around me won't let me lead a normal life and your lives don't revolve around me."

I told him I appreciated the car but I did worry about the perception the gift had created.

"Elvis you have touched our lives and we will never forget your friendship and generosity," I said. "However, when you are back in Memphis we will still be here in Denver doing our jobs and the press and some of our peers are already questioning why you gave us the cars."

Our conversation rehashed what Elvis and I had talked about before, both being dirt-poor kids and our struggles growing up and how other kids treated us poorly.

"Elvis we both know about discrimination," I said. "Kids make fun of you being poor and the clothes you wear."

Then we both talked about our dads being in jail and having to live with different relatives and going to different schools. When he spoke about his twin brother who died at birth, I shared the loss of my sister.

"I had a sister stillborn who is buried in the pauper section of a cemetery. It wasn't until years later that my wife and I had the money to have a marker placed on her grave."

We both became sentimental speaking about our pasts.

Elvis then shared that one reason he enjoyed our company is that he had always wanted to be a police officer, but God graced him with a singing voice.

He asked me what it was like being a cop and I explained that I had wanted to be a cop from an early age to catch drug dealers who sell to people like my dad.

I said if I had his voice, looks and could dance like him, I would have been an entertainer. Finally, I got Elvis to laugh a little but very little and I knew he was still upset.

"Elvis, you should know how important it is to know why people do what they do; including giving you gifts with no strings attached, which is highly unusual," I continued to explain. "I surely didn't mean to offend you."

Elvis said he understood but he had never been questioned before when he gave someone a gift.

I shared with him a deep question I kept in my heart.

"I've always thought about why I was so fortunate to meet you Elvis. I know it was Jerry who introduced us, but why have you continued to allow me to be around you? I am not complaining, I've had a good time. But, I am worn out keeping your ungodly hours."

Once more, a smile started to fade the anger in his face and I continued to explain why I questioned the car.

"Elvis I understand, Jerry and Ron are both great friends and cops. Me, I am just me - and I can say the damndest things without thinking first."

He listened to me and then tried to make me understand the car was truly a gift.

"Captain, Ron and you are all different, but none of you are like the others around me. None of you care if I do not give you anything, nor do you ask. You guys are true friends."

Elvis then brought up when we were in Vegas. "After the concert you were sitting on the stairs overlooking the dance floor watching others dance. I saw you and sat next to you. I pointed to a case of mineral water next to the stairs and asked if you would get me a bottle. You turned and asked me if I put my pants on the same as you do and I said yes, and you told me to get my own damn water and while I was at it get you one."

I thought, oh shit, I had hoped he would have forgotten that. Elvis started laughing and said no one else would say that to him.

"Bob you just say what you think and don't care if I am Elvis, the Colonel or whoever," Elvis said.

Then he brought up the time in Vail when he asked for one of my cigars and I gave him the last one in the box. I reminded him, it wasn't much, just a cheap cigar.

Elvis replied, "To me the Cadillac is not much."

It got to the point where were both were talked out. Elvis stood up and I left the room, neither one of us apologizing.

Jerry asked me about our conversation and I explained what happened.

Elvis then came fuming out of his room and told his pilots to gather up their things and that they were leaving immediately for Graceland. They asked about collecting his luggage in the hotel but he said leave it and someone would get it later.

Ron had just arrived at the hotel and encountered Elvis when he was leaving. Ron pressed Elvis on why he wanted to leave so soon.

"I don't want any implication made that I expect something from you guys in return for the cars," Elvis said. "I just think it is best if I left right now."

Captain Kennedy told me that after Elvis got back to Graceland he called him and said that I had really insulted him by thinking that he would ask for something in return for the Cadillac.

Obviously, Elvis hadn't really heard my explanations so Jerry told him that being overly suspicious made me a good narc. Jerry also told him that the way I grew up made me cautious before I could trust anyone.

Elvis cooled down and said he just had never been questioned before when he gave gifts because he had a line of people wanting something from him.

I felt badly that his vacation to Colorado ended on a sour note but I still have no apologies for my suspicions about the car. I was being honest about how I felt and I had hoped Elvis understood the reasons why I felt the way I did.

Elvis would make an unexpected trip back to Denver just a week later and any hard feelings had disappeared.

Chapter 8
ELVIS IN DENVER FOR DETECTIVE EUGENE KENNEDY'S FUNERAL
January 27, 1976

Elvis and Chief Dill
Elvis in Denver for Funeral 1976

Elvis delayed his scheduled recording sessions at his studio in Graceland when he received word that Captain Jerry Kennedy's brother ended his life on January 25, 1976.

Thirty-six year old Eugene 'Gene' Kennedy was a veteran Denver Police Detective who Elvis had met in Vegas when we were there for Elvis' concert in January 1971.

Eugene T. Kennedy
Investigator, Detective
Denver Police Department

He immediately got on his private plane and flew to Denver with a few of his entourage, including J.D. Sumner and members of the Stamps gospel quartet. They arrived on Tuesday, January 27, 1976.

Arrangements were made for Elvis to stay at the Regency Hotel, (now The Regency: Student Housing Community), 3900 Elati Street, just off Interstate 25 and Park Avenue, near downtown.

Regency Hotel

Gene was assigned to the Denver Police (DPD) Intelligence Bureau and on special assignment to the Colorado Organized Crime Strike Force (OCSF), and I was the sergeant designated as the OCSF Project Coordinator.

He was a great guy and always had a smile on his face. He was also a good police officer who everyone liked and respected.

When it became noticeable that Gene had developed a "drinking" problem, I tried many times to discuss this with him, I told him the drinking was impacting his work performance. Gene's peers and I were concerned with his well-being, but he assured us that he was only drinking when off duty.

Gene's consumption of alcohol finally resulted in his inability to function and I asked Chief Dill to reassign him to the Intelligence Bureau. Shortly after he was reassigned, Gene took his life.

Every time I drive by his house, which I do regularly, I second-guess myself about that reassignment. I also feel I should have done more, including ordering him to be evaluated for a 'fitness for duty.'

But Jerry Kennedy told me: "There wasn't anything you could have done Bob, to change Gene's drinking, he was having domestic problems."

Elvis didn't want to stand out at the funeral and he acquired a Denver Police dress blue uniform from a police uniform and equipment supply company. He had the uniform tailored-made with a double breast jacket and a made-to-order white dress shirt.

He wore the dress command officer's uniform to Gene's funeral with the gold Captain's badge affixed to the left breast of his dress jacket.

Elvis told us that he was wearing the police uniform to the funeral as a disguise to blend in with all of the other police officers that attended Gene's services, dressed in their formal blues.

Before attending Gene's recitation of the Rosary at Holy Family Parish on Tuesday, January 27, Elvis asked Jerry to find him a good barber because he needed a haircut. Ron called his barber, Danny Rupoli, at Fiore's Barbershop. Although, I only remember once having my hair cut by Rupoli, Jerry and Ron were frequent customers of Rupoli and knew him very well.

The following day, Gene's Mass of Christian Burial also was held at Holy Family and the pews were packed with an overflow turnout of DPD officers, other law enforcement officials, family members and friends.

Elvis quietly entered at the back of the church and although many in the crowd knew Elvis was there, they respectively focused on celebrating Gene's life and not meeting the superstar. That was exactly how Elvis wanted it.

JD Summer and the Stamps gospel group sang hymns at the funeral and to avoid a distraction, Elvis quietly exited from the back of the church to avoid a gathering.

We hurriedly ushered Elvis into our car and left for Jerry's brother, Phil Kennedy's home at 3929 Sheridan Blvd, a short distance from the church. Elvis wanted to be with the Kennedy family.

Before entering the house, Elvis handed me a small black jewelry box he had with him and asked me to keep it for him. I placed it in trunk of my car for security. Elvis retreated to the back bedroom with Gene's family members upon their arrival. He was very subdued and expressed his condolences many times. Elvis was very cautious not to take anything away from the grieving relatives but provided extra solace to them.

Elvis talked about his relationship with God and his loss of his mother. I was very impressed with his genuineness.

Me, Elvis, Ron and OCSF DPD Det. Bobby Simmons

We later returned to the Regency Hotel where Elvis met with Chief Dill, some of our wives and other officers who had attended Gene's funeral. I took a few photos while the group visited.

Elvis showing his Black Diamond ring to Jody and Joan

Elvis and Jody 1976

Jerry, Red West, Chief Dill and Elvis

Late into the night, Elvis got hungry and Ron suggested the Colorado Mine Company, a former restaurant in Glendale, a small community east of Denver. The restaurant was owned and operated by Buck and Cindy Scott, friends of Jerry and Ron.

Courtesy Denver Westword

Ron called to make sure the restaurant was still open and everyone got ready to leave the hotel. Captain Kennedy told DPD Officer Alta Metzinger that she would be staying at the hotel to watch Elvis' baggage, but it didn't feel right that she would miss out on the meal.

I asked Jerry to keep me at the hotel since I had luckily had other meals with Elvis and he agreed. Elvis wanted me to come but agreed I'd stay after he heard the reason why.

One of the workers at the restaurant was Nick Andurlakis, an Elvis fan who started his job there when he was sixteen years old.

Nick later became the owner of his own eatery, Nick's Cafe, 777 Simms St., in Golden, a community in the foothills west of Denver. In 2012, he recalled the night Elvis came to the Colorado Mine Company to the Denver newspaper, Westword.

Fools Gold - Nick's Cafe
777½ Simms St. Lakewood

Elvis - Peanut Butter Sandwiches - Nick's Cafe.

If you remember a few years ago, Graceland had the peanut butter sandwiches flown in from Denver, Co. to the Presidents Club Luncheon in Memphis! These were the same peanut butter sandwiches that Nick Andurlakis made for Elvis years ago. Nick was 16 years old at the time he met Elvis and worked for The Colorado Mine Co. The sandwich Elvis likes was called Fools Gold on the menu and cost $64.95, below in small print (price negotiable). Nick said Elvis came to the Mine Co. two times. Nick also delivered the sandwich to the Lisa Marie one time, which was parked on a runway at the airport in Denver. This is part of the story that J.D. Sumner told that they figured it out and it added up to $16,000 to fly to Denver that night and get the sandwiches and return to Memphis. Recently, The Expresley Elvis Fan Club of Denver went to Nicks Cafe and he fixed all of us the same sandwich the same way he fixed it for Elvis. In front of Nicks Cafe is a sign that reads, Parking for Elvis Only - Violators will be all shook up. The inside is also adorned with Elvis and other 50's stars of the era. Thank you Nick, and we love you Elvis.

by: Dee Shackley, The Elvis Fan Club of Denver Colorado

Nick and Kathleen Andurlakis at Nicks Café, decorated with Elvis memorabilia, August 9, 2012, photo courtesy of Mark Sanders and Dave Herrera Denver Westword News.

Nick said Ron asked him if he could stay past midnight to serve a special guest and Nick agreed.

"Eventually, I heard a knock on the back door. It was Pietrafeso; joined by a small army of other cops - all cops, it appeared, including police captain Jerry Kennedy," Nick told Westword. "I was friendly with many Denver officers, yet there was one I could not recall ever seeing before. Ron wanted to introduce me to someone. I see this man and think, 'Jeez, this looks like Elvis Presley. And it was Elvis. He was wearing a captain's uniform"

Elvis asked Nick what he would recommend on the menu.

"I was a pretty die-hard Elvis fan, and knew the King loved the peanut butter, jelly and banana sandwiches his mama used to make. So I suggested the Fool's Gold Loaf. The Fool's Gold Loaf was something that my colleagues at the restaurant and I came up with to add something completely offbeat to the menu. We had steak and lobster, but we had nothing 'fun' on the menu," Nick said.

"Fool's Gold Loaf was no ordinary sandwich: French white bread with smooth peanut butter, bacon, and grape jelly confined in the bread that was then heated. It was a ginormous, artery-hardening contraption invented and offered exclusively at the Colorado Mine Company." Nick told me.

Photo by Dave Herrera Denver Westword
You can still order a Fool's Gold Loaf sandwich at Nick's Café

After Elvis was introduced to the "Fools Gold Loaf" a legend was born.

The story of the legend grew when the media reported Elvis liked the sandwich so much, that when he craved the massive concoction he sent his private plane to pick up a Fool's Gold Loaf and fly it to Graceland.

It was in the early morning hours of January 29, when Elvis and the others returned to the hotel.

I had locked the door while guarding the baggage and had fallen asleep. The knock woke me up. I checked the peephole before opening the door to Elvis, Jerry, Ron and Elvis' bodyguards who collected the baggage.

Elvis said they were leaving and would like Jerry, Ron and me to come back with him to Memphis. Elvis said it was Lisa Marie's birthday and it would great if we could come celebrate her birthday at Graceland.

Ron told Elvis we had already made plans to be in New Orleans to give a presentation, 'On the Role of Investigators With Prosecutors' for the National College of District Attorney's. Elvis said he would send his plane to New Orleans to pick us up and bring us to Memphis.

Jerry flew back with Elvis that night and Ron and I got ready for our flight to New Orleans.

Elvis left without his jewelry box, which I later discovered still resting in the trunk of my car. I felt horrible I had forgotten to give it to him. Ron called Joe Esposito who said Elvis wasn't concerned and he would just pick up the jewelry box the next time he was in Denver. I put it back in the trunk of my car.

A couple of weeks later, Elvis came back to Denver because he was looking to buy a home in the Colorado Mountains. Jerry and I met him when he arrived at the airport on his private plane, the Lisa Marie.

When I gave him the jewelry box he said he was never worried about the jewels. He knew the box was in good hands. I thanked him for his confidence in me.

I was, however, anxious to know the contents of the box that I had been carrying around locked in my trunk.

When Elvis opened the box, I saw a bunch of items that looked like they were just thrown inside. I could tell it wasn't costume jewelry but the real stuff. Many of the items were of a religious nature.

Elvis thumbed through the box and picked up several pieces. He told us a short story about each piece he held.

He then grabbed what I believed to be the biggest and heaviest piece that shadowed the other jewels in the box: a Gold Lion Claw necklace. Elvis handed me the heavy necklace and I carefully placed it in Jerry's hands that handed it back to Elvis.

Elvis gave to me   The National Tattler

"This is yours Bob," Elvis said, handing the necklace back to me.

"Elvis, I appreciate the offer but are you sure?" I replied stunned by his generosity.

He stared at me, said he was sure he wanted me to have the necklace and continued to look at his other jewels.

He gave Jerry a very beautiful necklace of Jesus' face and head, something I would wear. I was very appreciative of the Lion Claw necklace but wasn't sure it was my style.

I later sold the necklace to Elvis' friend, Jimmy Velvet. I was told the necklace might have been part of the items stolen by burglars who broke into Jimmy Velvet's Elvis Presley Museum on September17, 1982 and took more than $1 million in jewelry, including diamond rings and necklaces.

Nowadays, we often don't read about the part of Elvis who was compassionate and generous. When he heard that Jerry's brother had died, Elvis showed true compassion by coming to the funeral. When he knew I felt badly about forgetting to give him his jewelry box, instead of acting like a spoiled superstar Elvis first trusted me to keep the box and then gave me the Lion Claw necklace.

His actions went a long way to cement my respect for him.

Chapter 9
WITH ELVIS IN MEMPHIS

Elvis invited Jerry, Ron and I to fly back to Memphis with him. Jerry did. Ron and I told Elvis we had a previous training commitment in New Orleans, Louisiana. Elvis said he understood and assured us to expect his pilot, Milo High, to pick us up after the conference and fly us to Memphis.

Ron and I arrived early January 29, 1976 in New Orleans. We grabbed a taxi to the hotel where the National College of District Attorneys (NCDA) training conference was being held. Since we would leave the conference as soon as our lectures were over, we left our luggage at the hotel front desk.

After our presentation and dinner with the attendees, we grabbed our luggage and left for the airport. It was late when Elvis' JetStar, named Hound Dog II flown by Milo, landed on the tarmac at Moisant Field. Milo and Jerry got off the plane and stretched before greeting us. Then we all got back on the plane for the return trip to Memphis.

Milo had his car parked at the airport and dropped Ron and I off at the Tennessee Howard Johnson motor lodge, 3280 Elvis Presley Blvd so we could check into our rooms that Joe had reserved for us. Milo took Jerry back to Graceland where he had been staying.

Howard Johnson Motor Inn Memphis

After some needed shut-eye, Joe arrived at the motor lodge. We visited for a short time before Joe drove us to Graceland. When we went inside Graceland the recording session Elvis had delayed to attend Gene Kennedy's funeral in Denver, was ready for the King to begin. His police guests were at Graceland so the recording session will need to be put on hold for a couple more days.

With the time I had to linger since I was now on Elvis' time, he was still sleeping, I strolled around the grounds of Graceland and had a familiar chat with Uncle Vester at the famous iron gates that kept Elvis safe from the public. Nothing had changed since I was previously at Graceland. Elvis devotees were lined up staring through the gates and those tall enough were looking over the concrete wall.

I told Uncle Vester, "Some of these folks look like the same ones I saw when I was here previously."

Uncle Vester said, "Yep, I'm on a first name basis with a lot of them and you are right, a few camp out with sleeping bags for days just hoping to get a glimpse of Elvis. Fans also write messages to Elvis on the stone wall. I hire a company on a regular schedule to clean the wall so that Elvis doesn't see the scribbles."

Knowing when Elvis was at Graceland was a question I had to ask a diehard Elvis devotee. I moved away from Vester to a young man barely being able to see over the stone wall. I asked him, "How do you know if Elvis is at Graceland?" He explained that he had contacts at the Memphis airport. When "Lisa Marie" would land, his friend who worked where the plane parks to unload, watched who got off and let him know if he sighted Elvis. I told him, "you guys have one-hell of an intelligence network."

I left the gate area and worked my way back to the house.

It was awesome to see the essential devices RCA had set-up that Elvis would need in recording professionally. Growing up, my dad recorded homemade records on a small recorder with a hand held microphone. Unfortunately, what tools he had at his disposal didn't counter his drug intoxicated slurred vocals. He would never break into the big time. Because of his drug dependency, when not in jail, he was on the run.

I moseyed downstairs to the "Jungle Room" where I found Jerry and Ron chatting with Elvis' guitar player, Charlie Hodge. I was first introduced to Charlie in 1970 and he was quiet except when he'd break out laughing at Elvis' humor. He wasn't restrained when I would ask him about himself. Charlie would tell me his southern upbringings and army stories. He was confident in his ability as a guitar player, and had a right to be. He was good.

One of Elvis' Gospel singers, J.D. Sumner was also chilling in the "Jungle Room." He said he just unwinding and loafing, killing time until the recording session started.

J.D. was always respectable and I appreciated his sets of belief and authenticity when he sang Gospel. Elvis told me once that this was the quality he most admired in J.D

I politely asked J.D. if I could bother him with a question on how he could get his voice to go so low.

I shouldn't have been startled when he said, "You bet."

J.D. told me to cup my right hand and place it over my right ear. He asks if I knew "How Great Thou Art." I said yes.

What came out of my mouth did not sound anything close to J.D., who told me it would take more than one lesson.

"I was not blessed to be a singer," I told J.D. Jerry loudly said, "Bob, don't give up your day job."

Finally, when Elvis emerged from his bedroom everyone was at his beck and call. Elvis said, "Let's play some racquetball."

Since we were at Graceland last, he had built a racquetball court fitness center behind his house and no longer had to go to Memphis State College.

I was first to try a game with Elvis. I didn't last long. When Elvis played racquetball his demeanor changed. He would swing the racquet with all his might. His swing was similar to how I had to use my police nightstick when apprehending a resisting suspect.

Back of Graceland, Racquetball court far right

It appeared to me that Elvis was releasing anger that had built up inside him. When Elvis went to grab a towel to wipe the sweat from his head, Jerry came over to me and said, "Hey Bob, it is my turn." Okay, I eagerly agreed. When Jerry passed by me he quietly said, "Bob I could see this was going to cause something ugly to happen and we are EP's guests." I replied to Jerry, "Great, I didn't want to be the victim of being hit by the ball that Elvis rocketed."

Jerry told Elvis that Bob would prefer to spend his time trying out his exercise equipment.

When we all left the court Elvis stopped to admire his horses and proudly talked about each one of them. Ron was the only one that understood what Elvis was saying. I told Elvis I was going to walk around the grounds again; there is real peace and quiet here, yet so close to his street (Elvis Presley Blvd.).

Elvis' horses behind Graceland

I had just passed Elvis' Pink Cad and was heading down the tree lined lane enjoying the landscape when all of a sudden I heard some noise behind me. I looked back and saw Lisa Marie driving a golf cart, looked like a small jeep, behind me. I jumped next to one of the many trees than lined the paved drive to get out of her way.

Elvis' pink and white Cad parked at Graceland

I stood and watched her pushing the pedal to the metal. She could sure maneuver it at her age of 8yrs.

Elvis said he had bought this pink and white oversized golf cart for Lisa Marie. I thought what fun my own kids would have with this.

When I would see Elvis with Lisa Marie it was moving to see how much he loved her. In his eyes she could do no wrong. I told Elvis that I understood, my wife tells me that I don't think our kids can do no wrong, because I'm not with them as much as she is, with me working all of the time. Elvis said this was one of his biggest regrets, being on the circuit so much and not seeing Lisa Marie more often.

I walked over to Jerry, who had heard Elvis and me talking, and said, "Jerry, Elvis really is a normal person like us."

It was late afternoon when Jerry, Ron and I were relaxing in high-back red chairs in Graceland's dining room. Elvis came halfway down the stairs from his bedroom and asked to see me. Jerry asked me if I knew what Elvis wanted to speak to me about and the only thing I could think of was my lack of desire to play racquetball with him.

Ron and Jerry both feared a repeat of my heated discussion with Elvis over the Cadillac and insisted on going with me to Elvis' room.

"Fine with me," I said in a low voice, so Elvis couldn't hear. "He may push me down the stairs."

I walked into the bedroom while Jerry and Ron stood in the bedroom doorway.

I was startled to see the televisions in the room, including one that had a smashed screen from a bullet hole. Elvis was holding a 44 Smith Wesson (S/W) nickel-plated magnum revolver with a long barrel that looked like a cannon. He had another S/W identical to the one he was holding next to him. I looked at Ron and Jerry and quietly said, "Oh shit."

When I asked him why he shot the TV, he said he didn't like the show that was on. I said, "Well Elvis that sounds like a good reason." Elvis laughed. I tried to smile but I admit I was a little concerned for my safety.

He picked up the other Smith Wesson next to him and handed it to me.

"Bob this one is for you and no, I am not asking you for anything in return," he said.

"Elvis, we are not here because we expect anything from you," I replied.

Jerry sensed this was headed in the wrong direction and said the guns looked like the ones actor Clint Eastwood carried in his movies.

"You're right Jerry," Elvis said. "I bought these two matching 44-mag pistols after I saw the movie Dirty Harry."

That defused the tension and I would later thank Jerry for saving me again from self-destructing.

Elvis handed me a tan leather shoulder holster and told me it went with the gun. After making sure the gun didn't have any bullets, Ron helped me put on the holster. The weight of the gun caused the holster to suspend down to my mid right knee. I was just too short.

Elvis saw me check the gun chamber for bullets.

"Bob, you don't think I would hand you a loaded weapon, do you?" Elvis said.

I told Elvis it was part of my police training to check if a gun is loaded but Elvis wasn't convinced.

"Jerry, does Bob trust anyone?" Elvis asked.

Then Jerry revealed an embarrassing moment in my life.

"I don't think he trusts himself, you know he shot himself in the foot one time," Jerry said, laughing.

Ignoring Jerry's comment, I focused on the weight of the gun in the holster.

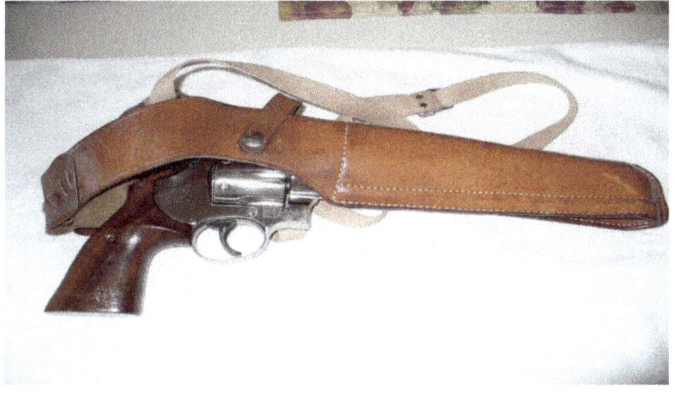

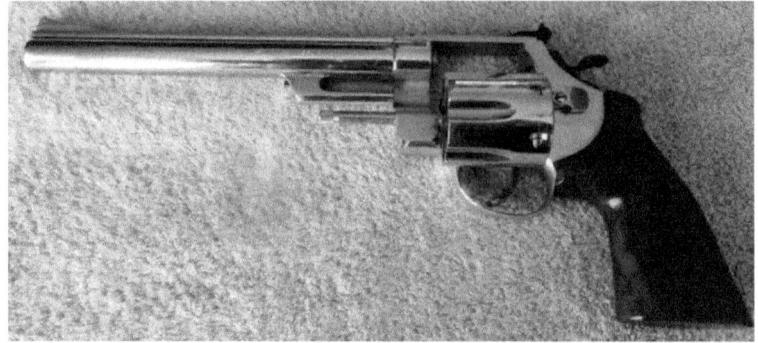

44 S/W Mag Elvis gave me

I told Elvis, "I could just see me wearing this to work and trying to run after someone. On the other hand it would surely scare the hell out of someone. It did me."

"That's what I got them for, to scare anyone that might want to come at me," Elvis said.

Elvis then turned his attention to his closet. He got off his bed and swung open the closet and started working through the garments. Elvis took one jacket at a time out and handed one to Jerry, then Ron and me.

He told us the jackets weren't worn often and he wanted us to have them because they no longer fit him.

I tried a few on and none fit.

"They don't fit, you're taller than me," I told Elvis. "Jerry is the only one close to your size. They don't call Ron and me 'Mini-Narcs' for no reason."

Elvis was amused and said, "Bob, you'll grow into them."

Then before I knew it, my mouth was getting the best of me again.

"Yeah, right and if you would lose some weight the jackets would fit you again," I said.

Elvis and Jerry saw no humor in this comment and Elvis advised us to clear out because he was going to change clothes and would see us downstairs.

Elvis can be stubborn and so can I but Jerry encouraged me to accept the gifts without further comment. I carried four coats, a gold key chain Elvis said once held the keys to his pink Cadillac, the 44-mag and the shoulder holster downstairs and was thankful that no one was around to see this. At least the key chain fit in my pocket. I needed these jackets like a hole in the head.

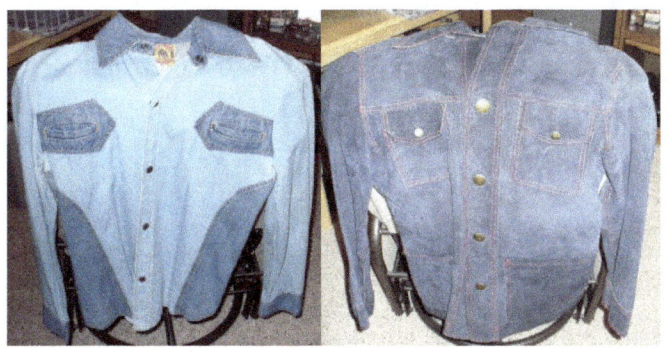

The Four Jackets Elvis gave me at Graceland

When we got downstairs, Jerry reminded me to think before I spoke. Even though Jerry also wondered about Elvis' weight, he was smooth enough not to say anything.

That evening Elvis took Jerry, Ron and me for a ride in his shiny black Stutz Blackhawk sports car and we got pulled over by the Memphis police for speeding. Elvis got out of the Blackhawk wearing his DPD blue Captain's uniform and chomping on an unlit cigarillo.

Elvis Stutz Blackhawk parked at Graceland

The two officers immediately recognized Elvis and called him Mr. Presley. Elvis was very respectful and didn't try to persuade the officers to not give him a ticket, but said he was showing some Denver Police Officers around Memphis.

Jerry got out of the car while Ron and I pushed ourselves out of the cramped back seat of the Blackhawk. Elvis was introducing us to the officers when they got a call over the police radio of a robbery in progress.

The call gave me an adrenaline rush. I hurriedly walked over to the cruiser and listened to the police dispatcher that the suspects were headed east on some street I don't remember.

The officers told Elvis they had to hurry off and to slow down, and they were glad to meet us. The officers were very professional, and I truly believe they would have written Elvis a ticket for speeding if they hadn't had the robbery to deal with.

I was glad Elvis listened to the officers and drove more slowly back to Graceland. The Denver media had questioned the cars Elvis gave Jerry, Ron and me, so I could see the headlines, "Three Denver cops with Elvis dressed in a DPD uniform were stopped for speeding in Memphis."

The next day, Elvis drove us on an unpaved road behind Graceland just north of where his horses grazed. He showed us a home he had bought for his girlfriend, Linda Thompson, the former 1972 Miss Tennessee who we had met in Vail.

Linda stayed with Elvis at Graceland while we were there and was always friendly. She was a beauty, inside and out, and truly a "southern belle." Linda, in my opinion, was the most attractive, polite, and down-to-earth woman Elvis was fortunate to call his girlfriend.

The times I was around Linda I noticed she was truly admired and respected by Elvis' entourage.

When we parked at her house, I wasn't surprised that it wasn't a mansion but rather a home that fit her humbleness. She met us at the door and graciously invited us in. There were houseplants all over but neatly organized.

Early the next morning, around 2 a.m., Elvis wanted to go to the movies to see "One Flew Over The Cuckoo's Nest." He rented the entire Memphian movie theater to do this. He told us this is where he had met Linda. Jerry, Ron and I sat down a few rows in front of Elvis. He kept throwing popcorn and laughing at us through the movie to keep us awake.

Elvis dropped Ron and I at the hotel and Elvis told us the Hound Dog would take us back to Denver tomorrow. Didn't happen, Elvis had other plans.

We both slept in later than usual because of the early-morning movie and knowing Elvis wouldn't be up and around till late afternoon. I was grateful for the extra time to pack. I cushioned the 44 Mag between my new attire from Elvis. I borrowed some twine from the front desk and wrapped my bulging baggage that I couldn't get zipped.

I met Ron, with his oversize luggage, in the motel lobby. Joe soon arrived and took us to Graceland.

Elvis had asked us to visit Memphis this time partially to celebrate his daughter, Lisa Marie's, eighth birthday on February 1.

We wanted to get Lisa Marie something for her birthday and Linda Thompson took me, Ron and Jerry shopping. The three of us pooled our money – something like $10 a piece –, which was a chunk of money for us then.

Elvis surprised the three of us with expensive-looking gold wrist watches. The watch had a circular dial, bar chapters, day and date window and sweeping second within a yellow metal case. The bezel featured the "ELVIS PRESLEY" monogram and the watch was attached to yellow gold metal bracelets.

Elvis gave me this watch in Memphis

The watch dial was signed Mathey Tissot and the watch box read: "Designed for Elvis Presley by Harry Levitch Jewelers in Memphis, Tennessee."

Like the gold necklaces we received in Las Vegas, Elvis told us he gave the watches only to close friends and I felt honored by the gift.

The visit was not all fun and games because Elvis still had to focus on his recording session. I was in the "Jungle Room" one day listening to Elvis talk about what music he was going to record when I asked him about recording in Graceland compared to a regular recording studio.

Elvis said to record one song he usually goes through several takes before getting it right, which usually wears out his background singers. J.D. Sumner laughed from the bottom of his voice and said, "Yep, EP is right."

I was taking it all in when out of the blue Elvis said he was hungry. "I have wanted another one of those 'Fool's Gold' sandwiches ever since I had one in Denver at the Colorado Mine Company. It was the best," he said.

What Elvis wants, he gets, and Ron called the Colorado Mine Company. He asked if several "Fools Gold Sandwiches" could be delivered to Elvis' plane at SIA.

We needed to get back to Denver, but never thought we would be leaving around 1:30 in the morning.

Elvis' private plane loaded with The King, Jerry, Ron and I along with a few other people – was scheduled to arrive for the unusual take-out order.

Nick Andurlakis stayed past midnight to prepare the sandwiches and had specially placed them on silver trays. When we arrived at SIA the sandwiches were waiting. Elvis insisted that we all eat one. He didn't need to encourage me because I was hungry from the trip. Thank God there was plenty of mineral water on the plane to wash down the mounds of peanut butter on the sandwiches.

Everyone enjoyed a sandwich, including Elvis' pilots, and between bites we listened to Elvis and Jerry entertain us with their jokes. Every once in a while J.D. or another member of the entourage threw out a joke, too. When Jerry tells jokes they are funny, even if some are off-color. Elvis, on the other hand, told jokes that I often missed the punch line.

When everyone laughed at an Elvis joke that I didn't think was funny, I asked Ron if I missed the punch line. He told me just to smile and laugh because if I told a joke, they'd likely not get my humor either.

I had to walk around inside the plane just to stay awake. It was breaking daylight when I finally told Elvis thanks again for everything and I had a great time. Elvis hugged me and said we will do it again soon because he had an upcoming concert scheduled for Denver.

I left the plane wearing my gold watch and carrying my heavy overstuffed luggage. I loaded the luggage in my car, which I had parked at the airport when I departed to New Orleans.

I drove home playing over the events of the trip and storing the growing memories of my incredible time with Elvis.

Chapter 10
ELVIS' LAST CONCERT IN COLORADO
April 23, 1976

LINES OF ELVIS PRESLEY FANS BACK UP OUTSIDE McNICHOLS ARENA FRIDAY NIGHT
Persons arriving for Presley concert clogged every en-
trance to arena, while stands of Mile High Stadium, in
background, stood almost empty for Denver Bears' open-
er. Game was canceled in 8th inning because of weather.

When Elvis arrived in Denver for his concert on April 23, 1976, he was upbeat and excited to be in Denver. I didn't notice anything unusual with him except he was gaining weight, which I joked about with him. He was very sensitive about his weight. This was one time I felt bad about joking with Elvis and admitted it. Unknowing to me this would be Elvis' last performance in the Mile High City.

The concert took place at the McNichols Sports Arena, fondly called "Big Mac" and located near downtown across from the Mile High Stadium, home of the Denver Broncos. When a new football stadium was built, "Big Mac" was torn down to make room for a parking lot.

Joe Esposito arranged to get tickets for our wives and my wife, Jody, was anxious to see Elvis in concert again. She was no different than any other female Elvis fan that thought the

King was sexy and good looking. Elvis had charisma and charm and when he sang he made it seem like he was singing personally to every woman at the concert. But unlike the other women at the concert, Jody would get to speak with Elvis after the show.

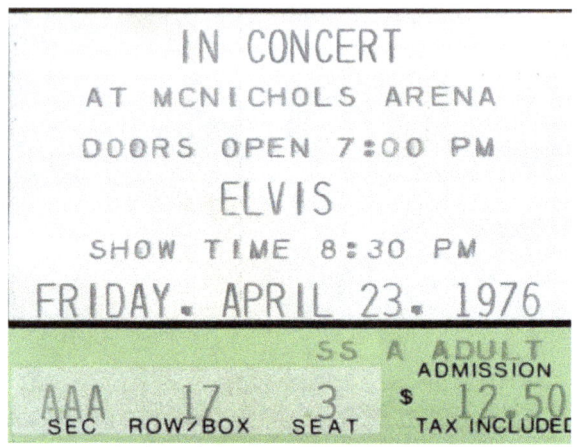

IN CONCERT

AT MCNICHOLS ARENA

DOORS OPEN 7:00 PM

ELVIS

SHOW TIME 8:30 PM

FRIDAY. APRIL 23. 1976

SS A ADULT
ADMISSION

AAA 17 3 $ 12.50
SEC ROW/BOX SEAT TAX INCLUDED

Jody's ticket stub from Concert

Following our familiar drill when picking up celebrities, Jerry had met with SIA officials and made arrangements to secure the COMBS tarmac where the "Lisa Marie" would arrive Wednesday, April 22, 1976.

When Elvis stepped off the plane, he looked like he had just wakened. He was wearing a cape and the DPD Captain's badge was pinned on it. He greeted each of us with a very sincere hug.

Joe Esposito hired a couple of limousines to take Elvis and his entourage to the Denver Hilton Hotel, downtown. Ron rode in one limo with Joe and others. Jerry rode with Elvis and three of his bodyguards. I drove my car to the Hilton ahead of the limos to alert officers stationed there that Elvis was on his way.

Hilton Hotel where Elvis stayed

Rooms were reserved for Elvis and his entourage and DPD officers working hotel security. Elvis' room was Room #2236, although he would occupy most of his time in Room #2228, where Jerry, Ron and I would retreat.

Chief Dill met us at the hotel and greeted Elvis when he arrived. Elvis and Jerry began rehashing some old stories.

Maybe these meetings had gotten too familiar because I realized, standing in the group, that I was bored. That feeling brought a little guilt because, what a way to feel when you are in the presence of a legend.

I had no clue where Joe and Ron were leaving to, but I wanted to go with them, but Jerry asked me to stay with him and Elvis. Jerry wanted me to keep check on the other two off-duty officers. They were in Room 2227 and their duty was to routinely check the lobby and parking areas.

I sat down in the suite, took a piece of Hilton stationery and a pen from the desk drawer and began to doodle. Elvis caught me drawing and looked down to see my sketch of a hand holding a cross.

My drawing Elvis liked

"Wow, Bob, you should pursue drawing more," he said.

I told him that I only doodle when I have time. Before I was married, I had a partial scholarship to the Colorado Institute of Art but there was no way I could come up with the remaining tuition. I was supporting my mother and a sister at the time.

Then Elvis blind-sided me again with his generosity and offered to pay for me to attend art school. I thanked him but said I honestly didn't have time, now with my work schedule and raising a family.

Elvis said, "I understand Bob but the offer is here."

While grateful for the offer, I also felt embarrassed, but I kept that to myself.

Elvis was always intrigued with criminal investigations OCSF (Organized Crime Strike Force) and continuously inquired about our work. He even asked to see photographs of our cases. We were very careful not to reveal any information to Elvis that could jeopardize a case. We had learned that Elvis loved to tell stories of what he had heard.

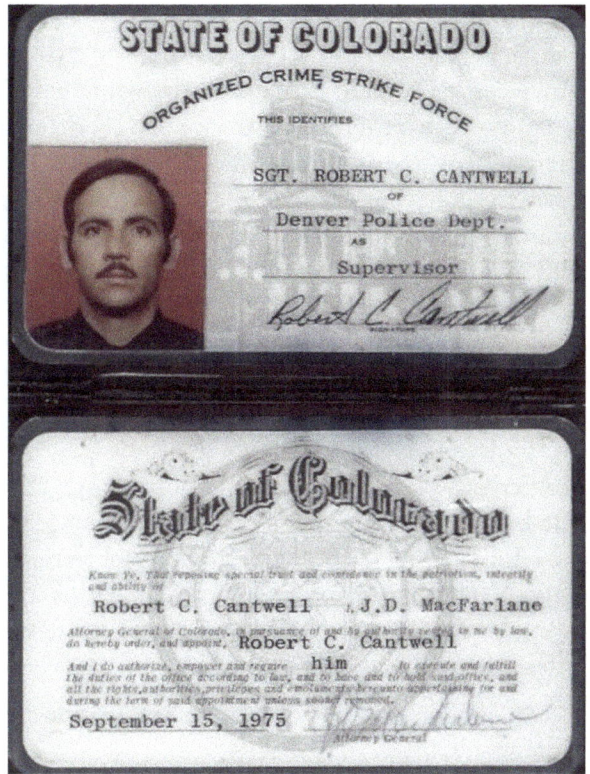

When I showed Elvis my OCSF credentials, Elvis wanted one. The Colorado Attorney General issued the credentials and arrangements were made for Elvis to obtain an OCSF Identification card.

We told Elvis that the funding of OCSF was in jeopardy. The Colorado State Legislature approved the funding but some lawmakers weren't convinced the strike force was necessary.

Elvis took his checkbook out, and before Ron or I could explain more about the funding, he was ready to write us a check for $400,000 to keep the OCSF operating. Ron and I explained we couldn't take the money because the decision on whether to fund the program needed to rest with the legislature.

"I will go and talk to them," Elvis said.

I convinced Elvis to wait a year and the topic was dropped. Somehow, a few legislators heard about Elvis' offer and said they wouldn't accept the money.

While we were at the hotel, J.D. Sumner introduced Elvis' back-up singers to me. Kathy Westmoreland, a tremendous vocalist who was very pretty and The Sweet Inspiration who definitely lived up to their name.

Where did time go? That first day with Elvis flew by and now it was the day of the concert. I was wearing my Sergeant uniform for my assignment to secure the hotel's parking garage where Elvis' limousines were parked.

Jerry was still DPD secondary (off-duty) work coordinator and assigned two of Denver's finest officers, who also happened to be brothers, to secure the hotel garage parking area with me. No one was authorized to be in this area unless they were on the list of names that Joe Esposito gave me and had Elvis identification passes.

DENVER   4/22/76

NAME
                            Room
          DIAL "7" + Room Number

JOE   ESPOSITO   2241

RED   WEST   7-2239

DICK GROB   2243

DAVE HEBLER   2233

CHARLIE HODGE   2235

VERNON PRESLEY 2244

AL   STRADA   2234

DAVID STANLEY 2232

DEAN NICOPLAS   2238

RICKY STANLEY 2230

DR. NICK   2231

Elvis   2236

SECURITY 2228   WARDROBE 224

The Denver Hilton.
(303) 893·3333

ELVIS PRESLEY SHOW - APRIL 1976

ROOM ASSIGNMENT LIST

JAMES BURTON	2201	26. LARRY STRICKLAND	1128
JOHN WILKINSON	2202	27. ED ENOCH S)	1137
JERRY SCHEFF	2203	28.. RONALD MABES S)	1141
RON TUTT	2204	29. MYRNA SMITH	1148
DAVID BRIGGS	2205	30. SYLVIA SHEMWELL	1152
JOHN RICH	2226	31. ESTELLE BROWN	1150
JACKIE KAHANE	2222	32. CLIFFORD ROWE	1138
KATHY WESTMORELAND	2223	33. KIETH LEE)	
JIM HAMILTON	2224	34. JEROME MONROE Twin-)	1122
BILL PORTER	2225	35. SHERRILL NIELSEN	1125
BRUCE JACKSON	1130	36. TOM HULETT	2210
TONY BROWN	1139	37. CHARLES STONE	2209
FELTON JARVIS	1050	38. ED BONJA	2211
JOE GUERCIO	no Show	39. MIKE BONJA)	
PAT HOUSTON	1041	40. RON JOHNSON Twin-)	2207
MARTY HARRELL	1030	41.)	
LOU DELL)		G. DROLET Twin-)	2220
RICHIE LA PORTE Twin -)	1027	42. BILL DISKIN	
ERNIE JONES)		43. RON BONJA Tw.}	2218
HOWARD STRUBEL Twin -)	1025	44. JEFF BONJA }	
DICK BURKE)		45. Richard DICK	2217
John Warner Twin -)	1023		
J.D. SUMNER	1024	*Security*	2227
BILL BAIZE	1126		
ED HILL	1112		

Unlike what had occurred at the Radisson Hotel in 1970, the Hilton did a great job not leaking that Elvis was staying there. This made our job easier in securing the 20th floor and the garage.

But as soon as I thought we'd have smooth sailing, we faced a problem and not because of Elvis' fans.

The garage elevator opened and a woman exited.

The two off duty DPD officers working me stopped her and asked for her identification explaining to her the reason. She told them that she was with Colonel Parker and had left her purse in his room.

The officers, who were detectives working off-duty in DPD uniforms, were very professional with the woman and repeatedly explained to her why she couldn't be in the garage. She became very agitated and started yelling,

"I am with Colonel Parker!"

So, I walked over to her and explained again that no one was to be in this area without proper Elvis identification.

She stood her ground and threatened to call the Colonel.

Since she wouldn't get back on the elevator and when there was no use continuing to reason with her, I physically picked her up and put her back in the elevator.

While one officer pushed the elevator's button to the lobby, she yelled, "The Colonel will have your jobs!"

It wasn't long before the elevator opened and out stepped the Colonel. I stepped forward and explained I had no choice but to physically remove the woman because she refused to leave and her name was not on the list.

The Colonel didn't say anything for a moment and I thought he may have recognized me from when Elvis asked me to tail him while he gambled in Las Vegas. I was right.

"I know you from being around Elvis, mainly in Las Vegas," he said. "It took me a minute because you are in uniform."

I told him he remembered correctly and he glanced at the two other officers who had my back.

The Colonel yelled that the woman was telling the truth, she was with him. I repeated that didn't matter because her name wasn't on the list. He said he was going to have me fired and wanted me out of the building.

I told him we were following orders and only the Captain (Jerry) could fire me. He went back into the elevator saying he was going to get Jerry. I told him, "Have at it."

I assured the two officers that we were just doing our job and we had handled it professionally. I told them I would speak to the Captain who I expected to arrive shortly.

He did, along with the Colonel and Elvis.

The Colonel pointed at me and proclaimed, "I want him fired!"

The Captain looked at Elvis and said, "Elvis, all the Colonel needs is a good jump."

That off-color comment sent Elvis into fits of laughter.

I thought Elvis was going to fall down because he was laughing so hard. The Colonel got madder because Elvis thought the comment was funny. The Captain pulled out a big cigar and told the Colonel to have a cigar and relax. The Colonel stomped off and got back into the elevator.

Still laughing, Elvis managed to say: "Great job!"

The Captain said he thought the woman was the Colonel's secretary but it still didn't matter because the Colonel should have added her to the authorized list.

Ron's brother, Bobby, a Jefferson County Sheriff's deputy was working off-duty for the concert and met us in the hotel garage. He recalled that evening in an interview with the Denver newspaper, Westword.

"I vividly remember doing security at the singer's final concert in the Mile High City. The King was nervous - scared, even - in the final moments leading up to the performance," Bobby told the newspaper.

Bobby was part of about six police vehicles that escorted Elvis to McNichols Arena. The vehicles were parked facing the exit to make a quick getaway after the show.

Bobby was doing normal security in the arena hallways when Elvis and Joe Esposito appeared. Joe ran back to the dressing room and Elvis and Bobby stood side by side.

"For just a couple of minutes it was like all these people disappeared, and it was just Elvis and me in that hallway. He's got on his white jumpsuit and all these scarves around his neck. He had his fists clenched and was looking down. Then he looked up at me and says, 'Are you nervous?' I said no. And he said, 'Yeah, I am. I really am.' And it struck me: Here's a guy who's been an icon since the '50s, has probably performed in front of millions, and he's nervous?"

As the nerves got worst, Elvis literally had to have people nearby help him to stand. When the opening act, the Sweet Inspirations, finished, the arena went dark.

Bobby recalled that once the curtains opened the place lit up with camera flashbulbs. The Rocky Mountain News reported that 19,000 people enjoyed the sold-out concert.

"If Elvis had seen his star fade, as many critics at the time suggested, it sure wasn't evident that night. The show ended, and the King was rushed away instantly," Bobby said. "I remember an Elvis crippled by the performance he had just given. When he was done, he was done. He had given so much energy that, when he got done, he felt like he'd been hit by a Mack truck."

Lots of fans brought items to give Elvis and he accepted a hand-painted coffee mug from one woman and gave it to me.

Elvis was still sweating when we arrived back at the Hilton. He took a blue scarf from around his neck and handed it to me along with a rose that was thrown on the stage. He told me to give both to my wife.

Before leaving the hotel, I went downstairs and asked the Hilton manager on duty for the key to Room 2228, where I had stayed while with Elvis, for a souvenir. I still have the key.

Jerry, Ron and I went with Elvis to the airport. Like many times before, I told Elvis "Vaya con Dios," (Go with God) as he hugged each of us and boarded his private plane, "Lisa Marie".

The last thing he said was that he would see us again.

I drove home exhausted by the evening and my wife, who left after the concert, greeted me with stars in her eyes. She was so excited and happy that she was able to go to the Elvis' concert. When I handed her the scarf and rose Elvis had given her, I swear she was as excited as a little kid and she has saved them all these years.

Rose and scarf Elvis gave my wife.

This visit was the last time I would see Elvis alive.

Chapter 11
ELVIS HAS LEFT–BUT FOR ME HE LIVES ON

Copies of the three news articles I purchased before leaving back to Denver

When I first heard the news on August 16, 1977 that Elvis had died, I thought it was some kind of a sick stunt. But then

Vernon Presley called Jerry and Joe Esposito called Ron and confirmed that The King really was gone. Jerry and Ron passed on the sad news and the awful truth left me stunned.

The Elvis Presley I knew had "left the building" for the last time at the age of 42. Jerry said he was told that Elvis retired to his bedroom at Graceland around 7 a.m. to rest before he was schedule to fly to Portland, Maine for a concert. When he was discovered unconscious, he was taken by ambulance to Baptist Memorial Hospital and he was pronounced DOA (Dead on Arrival).

Elvis' death was the lead story on every radio and television station, nationally and internationally. Tears were flowing all across the world and would continue for months and years after.

I felt the news media wouldn't let Elvis' overwhelming popularity continue; they needed "dirt," and found those who would provide them the stories they were looking for. At times I caught myself believing some of the accusations. I replayed all the times I was with Elvis and examined if I may have missed something.

I thought no I would have surely noticed if Elvis was strung out like others had reported. Jerry, Ron and I were trained experts on identifying addicted drug users and we never would have turned a blind eye if Elvis exhibited the signs.

Elvis' father, Vernon, and Joe Esposito requested we come to Memphis. We grabbed the first flight we could book-seats on and headed to Memphis. We arrived late August 16.

Joe made reservations for us at the Howard Johnson's near Graceland, where we had previously stayed before. The motel was close to Graceland and Elvis was well known to the motel staff: Elvis had stayed there when Graceland was being remodeled.

We were very lucky to have reserved rooms because Elvis' grieving fans and the news media flooded into Memphis and were looking for rooms close to Graceland.

I brought my best clothes to Memphis, dark blue dress pants and a black and white striped sport jacket. I knew Elvis wouldn't have wanted me to go buy a new suit because of all of the talks we'd had about growing up poor and him knowing I was raising a family on an officer's pay.

After I dropped my bag in my room, I met Jerry and Ron, who were already waiting with Joe in the motel lobby for me. Joe drove us to Graceland, carefully maneuvering the traffic jams and the crowds of people already gathering at the front gate. Some fans tried to scale the wall, but the Memphis Police were there to keep them back.

Inside Graceland, Elvis' family and friends gathered to pay their respects. Elvis' grief-stricken father greeted us and thanked us for coming.

Vernon said with tears, "Elvis always talked about the respect he had for you as true friends." And then he asked us to help him stand guard over Elvis' body.

I whispered to Jerry that I thought he wanted him and Ron because I was sure the Colonel would not want me around after our dust-up in Denver. Jerry assured me Vernon meant all of us but asked me to avoid getting into any trouble. But sometimes trouble just follows me without being invited.

The room where the piano was when I was there before was removed and replaced with Elvis' draped copper casket. I walked over to the casket because I needed to satisfy myself that Elvis was really dead. Despite the confirmation from his family, like many others I was still skeptical that Elvis had died. I gazed into the casket and was transfixed when I saw the whitish make-up on his face.

I took in every detail and touched his hands, which were very cold and real. I no longer questioned the sad truth. Elvis had passed on from this world.

I felt like all eyes were on me when Jerry came over and we both stood together looking at Elvis and trying hard to disguise and control our emotions. There we stood watching over him in death as we had when he performed concerts in Colorado. Being cops you are expected to be tough and not show any feelings in public; afterwards is when you express your feelings in solitude.

It was very hot in the house and Elvis' dad asked me to make sure no one stood in front of the front door because that's where a breeze was coming in. The door was open and there was a large man standing in front of the door. I went over to the man and explained Elvis' dad requested that no one stand in front of the door to block the airflow into the house. I politely asked him to move and he told me he was George Hamilton. I said I don't know you and it wouldn't matter any way if I did.

After some verbal exchange, he irately left and walked over to Mr. Presley. They spoke briefly but he didn't come back. I was sweating, not because it was hot, but because in all this grief I didn't need or want a confrontation with anyone.

Jerry was watching and came over to me. I told him what had happen.

"Jerry why me… Mr. Presley could have asked you or Ron." I said.

"You did exactly what Mr. Presley asked and I will handle it if there is a next time," he said.

Others must have been watching and thankfully no one else blocked the front door.

Sometime later (just to interject), I was working off-duty in uniform at Stapleton International Airport at the departure area for planes leaving and arriving from Aspen, which was just west of the main terminal. I was standing by the door where passengers enter when I spotted Mr. Hamilton, who I later learned was an actor. He was dressed in a big brown fur-looking coat and he was staring at me. When he started to walk toward me I turned my back to him and removed my nameplate from my jacket.

When he approached me he said, "Do I know you officer?" I wanted to say yes but settled for no. He said, "Well you sure look familiar." Thankfully, his flight was ready to board so he left. It was winter and yet he had as dark a tan as he had at Graceland.

While I was watching the front door, I saw a woman seated on the same staircase that had trailed Elvis to his bedroom on during our last visit to Graceland. She was bent over with her arms folded and her head on her lap. She was crying in a low tone and every once in awhile looked up from her lap.

I asked Ron who she was and he answered Elvis's girlfriend, Ginger, like I should have known her. But I had never met her.

Before we left Graceland for the Forest Hill Cemetery, there was a private service inside Graceland before the casket was closed so Elvis' family and friends could say a last good-bye to Elvis. There were a lot of tears. This was very emotional for me. I stood back and watched the mourners who would genuinely miss Elvis, including me. I cared about the true friendship with the man and not the gifts he gave me with no strings attached.

When Elvis' casket was being carried out the front doors of Graceland, it became very still and quiet, somewhat eerie to me, and then out of the stillness a limb fell from a nearby tree. I walked over and picked it up before leaving in the funeral procession and placed it close to the house.

Part of a limb that fell the day of Elvis' Funeral that I brought back to Denver

After returning to Graceland from the funeral, I picked up the limb and took it back to the motel. The limb was larger than my suitcase so I broke it to the size to fit in the suitcase. I broke a piece off and gave it to Jerry and broke off another piece for Ron.

I carried mine back with me to Colorado and still have it. I later learned from Joe Esposito that the limb came from a

Dogwood tree, which was one of Elvis' favorite trees at Graceland.

When we were ready for the funeral procession, there were an estimated 17 recently washed and shining white Cadillacs lined up behind the white hearse. Vernon Presley must have had a pecking order of who would occupy which limo. I was very honored when Jerry and I were seated, I believe, in the fifth or sixth limo in the procession.

Outside the gates, Memphis Police held back the crowds of Elvis fans screaming "Elvis-Elvis-Elvis!" The paramedics were kept busy by some fans that actually fainted from the emotions and the many hours they kept vigil.

When we exited onto Elvis Presley Boulevard I saw a sea of people in the streets trying to get a glimpse of the casket inside the hearse.

Although it slowed the trip to the cemetery, I believe the Elvis I knew would have wanted this for his last performance in front of all of his loyal screaming fans. If he could have, he would have thrown scarves.

At the funeral, Jerry, Ron and I were not far behind the casket as it was ushered into the chapel by the pallbearers. It was fitting for Gospel singers Jake Hess and J.D. Sumner to sing. Elvis always talked about these two and how he never tired listening to them. I felt the same way about their music.

Jake Hess sang, "Known Only to Him," that brought chills to me and I am sure to others. I heard Mr. Hess sing Gospel songs before but not as touching as this time. Whenever I watched him later when he was on the Bill Gaither Homecoming Hour, he always brought back my memories of Elvis' funeral.

After the services, we returned to Graceland. Some of the mourners continued on to their planned destinations. I had some extra time before leaving for our flight back to Denver and me and Marie Dill (Art Dill's wife) took a last look at Graceland and snapped some memorable photographs.

Me, Ron and Jerry at Graceland- taken after Elvis' Funeral

Jerry admiring some of the flowers delivered at Graceland

Me and Marie Dill

I read where every floral shop in Memphis and surrounding areas sold out all the flowers they could mustard up for Elvis' funeral. I believed it when I saw the hundreds of bouquets at the funeral and those at Graceland.

When Jerry, Ron and I departed Memphis, we left with heavy hearts.

Some people may not understand our relationship with this celebrity who was often misunderstood in life and perhaps misrepresented in death. But it was pretty simple for us then and now.

I regard Elvis Presley as one of the most important individuals I have met in my lifetime and one who I continue to call a "friend.

Elvis' bus parked at Graceland during the funeral

Chapter 12
CONCLUSION
THE AFTERMATH

Elvis, Jerry, Ron and me

November 17, 1970, was the beginning of the good, the bad and the ugly. Meeting and knowing Elvis was the good. Regretting I didn't have more time with Elvis was the bad. The aftermath of dealing with all of the allegations reported by the media and jealous peers was the ugly.

As I mentioned previously, Elvis didn't act like most celebrities who needed off-duty police security for events in Denver. He was far from being a diva.

The Elvis I knew was a superstar and authentic country gentleman who cherished being around those that regarded him as an ordinary person. I got a glimpse of his anger over our discussion about the Cadillac and he likely lost his temper on other occasions as well – like anyone does.

But Elvis shattered my ability to stereotype entertainers, which usually I was right on.

That stereotype was dead wrong with Elvis. Elvis became a friend and touched my life as well as the lives of Jerry and Ron. Although Elvis has passed, I have not forgotten him.

I also have not forgotten what I felt were inappropriate questions from the media after Elvis' death. One call came from a reporter at an eastern newspaper and he asked about Elvis' drug problem.

The question lit my fuse and he got an earful…

"I had never seen Elvis use or under the influence of drugs," I told the reporter. "I've been in narcotic enforcement for many years, and witnessed my own dad plastered on drugs. I can tell if a guy is using drugs just by looking at him. If Elvis did, he sure as hell didn't do it around me. You show me the proof that Elvis was on drugs around me. Until somebody does, I won't believe it and the official cause of Elvis' death was reported as heart failure. If anything, Elvis overdosed on greasy food, hamburgers and 'Fools-Gold' sandwiches."

Only God knows the truth about Elvis' life. I know Elvis didn't compromise my principles, integrity, or ethics. But the friendship did cause a lot of envy with my peers and others who believed the media. A colleague in the police department, who I thought was a close friend, was so envious that our friendship deteriorated.

Probes into Elvis' association with Jerry, Ron and me didn't end after his death. The Colorado Legislature and Denver Police ethics boards convened to look into the gifts Elvis gave us and our trips with him.

One year after Elvis died I was appointed to attend the prestigious FBI (Federal Bureau of Investigations) N/A (National Academy), Class 112. Prior to leaving for the N/A the

Denver Office of the FBI contacted me and said they had received a letter from a Denver Police officer, who they wouldn't identify, regarding my receiving a Cadillac from Elvis. The letter also claimed that I should have known that Elvis was a drug addict because I was a NARC.

I told the FBI everything I knew and asked them to contact anyone they wished. I knew they had already conducted a neighbor canvas and reviewed my prior employment history as part of a background check.

The FBI was very methodical. I added some others they may want to talk to, including Joe Esposito. The FBI got back to me and said that every one they talked to told them, that if I knew Elvis used drugs I would have arrested him, regardless of his status as a celebrity. The FBI concluded after talking to many people that they could find nothing to prevent me from attending the N/A.

I was approved and only had a short time to travel to the FBI training facilities in Quantico.

The Manager of Safety, who oversaw the Denver police, also conducted a review. His ruling stated: "I see nothing wrong with the acceptance of the gifts by the officers. When you tell a policeman that he can't do anything an ordinary person can, then you've made the officer a second-class citizen. The gifts from Presley were clearly made as a result of the singer's friendship with the three officers who did security work for him while off duty."

State legislators also questioned Ron and me about the trip we took to Memphis as Presley's guests when we left New Orleans. They incorrectly claimed we had charged the state for the plane tickets and per-diem for the time we left New Orleans to Memphis.

We were able to show them our expense forms. Thankfully, I keep everything which revealed we didn't charged any expenses from the time we left New Orleans for Memphis through the flight back to Denver. Since we took personal time it actually saved the National College of District Attorney's money.

But later when Elvis' private doctor, who I had met, was charged with 14 counts of abusing his license to prescribe controlled drugs to Elvis and faced prison time, I started questioning my narc skills.

Yet despite all the reports of drug use, I knew in my heart I did not ignore anything just to be around Elvis.

The trial for Dr. Nick began in October and after a month the jury concluded that he had tried to act in the best interests of his patient. He was acquitted on all counts. But another medical board review resulted in him losing his license.

Seventeen years after Elvis' death, and thousands of headlines about his reported drug use, another inquiry into the cause of death was done in 1994. "There is nothing in any of the data that supports Elvis' death from drugs. In fact, everything points to a sudden, violent heart attack," coroner Dr. Joseph Davis reported

The front pages of The Denver Post, Rocky Mountain News and television stations reported on the inquiries into our friendship with Elvis and the gifts he gave us. This was very tiring however; Journalists – like detectives – are suspicious and perhaps look for the worst in a situation. They reported on the sensational side of the Elvis story – but there was so much more about the man they never saw.

Jerry, Ron and I were cleared of any wrongdoing accepting Elvis' gifts: but still questions lingered.

This is my story of The Elvis I Knew.

Rocky Mountain News

Meet the Author
Robert C. Cantwell

When I saw that the Denver Civil Service Commission was hiring police officers in 1964 for the Denver Police Department (DPD), this was my chance to be what *I* always dreamed of being since a very early age - a cop!

The age limit for an officer had been lowered from 22 to 21 and the height to five-foot-nine and no college degree was required. I met the qualification but could I pass the written exam?

I had attended five different high schools because my dad was on the run from the law and bill collectors. The only way I was able to achieve a high school diploma was because Ds were a passing grade. My classmates said that the only higher education I would obtain would be through the Department of Corrections. It would astonish them if they knew today that I have obtained an Associate Degree and a Bachelor's Degree.

Although I was working two jobs to support my wife and newborn daughter, Dawna, I found time to study the "ARCO Patrolman Test Preparation Study" guide prior to the scheduled written test on March 5, 1964.

When I arrived for the test I panicked and started to turn around and go back home. I wondered how I could compete with the large number of applicants. I was petrified and feared the embarrassment of failing.

I stood by the entrance of the building where the exam was taking place just until a uniform officer came over. He was checking everyone who entered to be sure they were on the list for the test. He confirmed my name was on the list.

As I looked at the other applicants in the building, I felt out of place. Most of them were dressed in shirt and ties. I wore a pair of jeans.

But my jeans were nice and clean because my wife, Jody, always made sure my clothes were presentable – even thought she had to often patch them.

My two jobs of digging and crawling in ditches for the Water Department and pumping gas and changing oil didn't require new clothes.

The officer asked if I was okay. I said I was just nervous. The officer told me that everyone who wants the job bad enough is nervous. He said some are just taking the test because they need a job. Others wanted to be a police officer because their dad or granddad was a cop. Others just wanted the power that goes with the badge and some applied for the excitement of the job.

The officer's words calmed me down and gave me encouragement to take the test and not back out.

I knew faith got me here. I sat down and said a quiet prayer: "God if this is this what you prepared me for, let me pass."

When I received a letter that I had successfully passed the written test and I was scheduled for the Physical Agility Test for April 15. I wasn't concerned about this test. I had boxed in the Golden Gloves and kept in shape with one of my jobs carrying 12-inch cast-iron pipes in and out of ditches. I successfully passed and then was scheduled for a Polygraph Examination on May 2.

The polygraph made me a little nervous. What if they asked me questions about my dad? What about when I was a youngster in Texas and had stolen some food to feed my mom and sisters? Would they care that I had to drive a motor bicycle to work with no license plates, which I often had to pedal because the engine didn't always work?

Should I be concerned when DPD Chief of Police Harold Dill requested I come to his office?

The chief asked me where I lived. I told him Jody and I had just gotten married and rented the basement apartment from a man, his wife and their small daughter who lived in the upstairs. I answered all of the questions honestly. The DPD was still reeling from a scandal involving officers who were stealing. The man who lived upstairs was a DPD sergeant and I did notice he had a lot of new tires in the garage he wouldn't let my wife or me use. I had peeked in and it was full of new tires.

I also honestly answered their questions about my dad and passed the polygraph. Next up was the Oral Interview on May 18. I responded to the board's probing questions successfully and entered the Police Academy on June 16.

Thus, I launched my career of more than 47 years in Law Enforcement.

I made Detective early on in my career and obtained another of my goals to investigate and arrest drug offenders.

I was promoted through every rank in the Denver Police Department. I also had a successful career as the Director of Prisons for the Colorado Department of Corrections and as the Director of the Colorado Bureau Of Investigation.

My wife and I would have two more children, Rob and Ron.

The scared kid who was afraid to take the police exam never dreamed he would personally meet a long list of famous people, including U.S. Presidents, Mother Teresa, the Beatles, Muhammad Ali, Bill Cosby, and a long list of professional athletes and others that I proudly hang on my wall including the King- Elvis Presley.

I rose above adversity with faith, dedication, determination, work ethic, and most of all support from my wife, Jody, who held   the   ladder   while   I   climbed   to   the   top.

OFFICE OF THE INSPECTOR IN CHARGE
P.O. Box 329
Denver. CO   80201-0329

January 15, 1993

Mr. Bob Cantwell
Division Chief (Retired)
Denver Police Department

Dear Mr. Cantwell:

The Denver Division of the Postal Inspection Service had 20 special commemorative Elvis stamps created to be issued to distinguished citizens who have worked with federal law enforcement. The stamps were hand cancelled January 8, 1993, Elvis' birthday, at the Denver Downtown Station.

You, sir, have been selected as one of the recipients of the 20 special commemorative stamps for your distinguished service to federal law enforcement. It is expected that the Elvis stamp will be the most popular stamp ever issued by the U.S. Postal Service. Three-hundred-million of the stamps have already been printed, about the twice the normal run for a commemorative stamp plate. Please accept this on behalf of the Postal Inspection Service as a token of our appreciation.

Sincerely,

John G. Freeman
Inspector in Charge

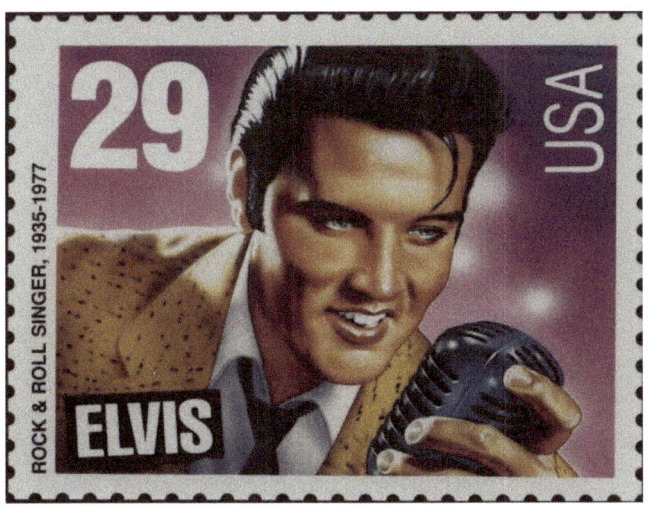

INDEX

Lightning Source UK Ltd.
Milton Keynes UK
UKHW050641271222
414429UK00008B/73